Spirituality and Poverty
in a
Land of Plenty

Spirituality and Poverty in a Land of Plenty

Imagining a Future without Poverty and Inequality in Ireland

Editors
Seán Healy, S.M.A.
Brigid Reynolds, S.M.
Tom Jordan, O.P.

CORI JUSTICE COMMISSION
in association with
DOMINICANPUBLICATIONS

First published (2004) by
CORI Justice Commission
in association with
Dominican Publications
42 Parnell Square
Dublin 1

ISBN 1-871552-92-3

Cover: from a painting by iconographer David O'Riordan,
a priest of the diocese of Cloyne.

Design by Bill Bolger

Printed in the Republic of Ireland by
The Leinster Leader, Naas, Co. Kildare

Contents

Introduction

As Chairperson of the Justice Commission of the Conference of Religious of Ireland (CORI) it is my privilege to welcome you on behalf of the Commission to this, the first annual conference on Spirituality for Social engagement. Today marks a historic occasion in the life of the CORI Justice Commission.

As you are aware, the Justice Commission has four programmes that are focused on delivering its mission and one of these programmes deals with Spirituality. [The others are Public Policy, Enabling and Empowering, Advocacy and Communication]. Spirituality has been a central element of the Justice Commission's work since its establishment 23 years ago.

The mission of the Justice Commission is fired by that of Jesus himself. He explained his mission with the words, 'I have come so that you may have life and have it to the full' (John 10:10). It is a gospel imperative that human beings are to enjoy fullness of life. However, for a variety of reasons many people today do not enjoy this outcome. Among the obstacles to enjoying the fullness of life are poverty, inequality and social exclusion. Jesus recognised this when he told his followers that he was sent 'to bring good news to the poor' (Luke 4:18).

For the past two thousand years the followers of Jesus have promoted fullness of life and sought to bring this good news to all people but especially to poor and excluded people. Each generation, as affirmed by the second Vatican Council has responded 'to the duty of scrutinising the signs of the times and of interpreting them in the light of the Gospel' (Vatican II: *Gaudium et Spes* n. 4). This continues to be a daunting responsibility for each one of us today, as followers of Jesus.

Indeed, it raises some serious questions for us: What is 'good news' for people today? What supports the present generation of Christians in scrutinising the signs of the times? How can we be authentic in interpreting these signs in the light of the

Gospel? What motivates and supports us in bringing good news to our sisters and brothers? These are among the questions we hope to address in this series of annual conferences.

Many of you will be familiar with our annual Social Policy Conference and you might be expecting the same format and structure. Today's conference is structured a little differently because we want to involve the wisdom and the experience of all present in teasing out the implications of what is being shared. Therefore, a) each of the presentations will be followed by a round-table discussion involving everyone. b) Each table will have a facilitator already designated. The facilitator will take their group through a series of questions aimed at drawing out the implications of the paper already presented.

Then, in the mid-afternoon, we will have an open forum with feedback from some tables and discussion with all the presenters of papers during the day.

The discussions at all the tables will be summarised by the facilitators and then put together and published in book form together with the papers of the conference. The book will also contain a study guide for use by individuals or groups who wish to study and reflect on the material contained in the book. This 'user friendly' book will be published jointly by Dominican Publications and CORI Justice Commission later this year.

So, today we specifically address the issue of Spirituality and Poverty in a Land of Plenty. In a column in *The Irish Times* last week Vincent Browne asked: 'Isn't there something revolting about a society that rewards some people so spectacularly and allocates such miserable rewards to so many others?' He was addressing the divisions in Irish society and the values that allow these divisions to persist. Indeed, these are some of the questions that we will address today.

For this, our first annual conference, we have gathered together some eminent speakers to help us in addressing these questions.

Theresa Kilmurray
Chair: CORI Justice Commission
27 April 2004

Foreword

It is accepted that family members look out for, and care for each other. This is seen as 'natural' and is expected as the norm. People who extend this care to include people living in their area are seen as generous and good neighbours. This sharing and caring makes for happy and vibrant communities which can provide some tangible rewards for the efforts invested. But what of people who are not related to us, people we have never met, people living in other towns or countries, should we care for them? What of other life forms, what of our environment, why should we care for it or make sacrifices that will not benefit us personally but will benefit the generations after us? In our work in Third World countries and later with the CORI Justice Commission, we have often asked why do people inconvenience themselves even to the point of risking their lives to improve the lot of people who will never know them let alone thank them for their efforts?

Under the general title of *Spirituality for Social Engagement* we wish to explore firstly, what motivates people to work for the improvement of others especially when this work takes them into areas that are uncomfortable, unpopular, career-threatening and even life-threatening? Secondly, when people make this choice what sustains them in their life and work?

Through discussion with friends and colleagues it was decided to explore these questions by looking at specific issues which make life difficult for some people. What are the structures that keep people in these situations? What motivates people to maintain these structures? Who are the people who are trying to change or transform these structures? What motivates this work for change and how are people supported in it? We believe that spirituality is key to understanding this motivation and action.

We favour a broad understanding of spirituality. For us

spirituality is the 'habitual stance' of the person; it is what shapes and moves the person and influences her/his relationships. These relationships are many and varied. They include relationships with self, people, institutions, environment and the Transcendent. This is a dynamic and inclusive understanding of spirituality that recognises that every person has a spirituality. Spirituality influences all our decisions and actions. Whether this spirituality is acknowledged and how it is articulated will vary with the person. There are many traditions of spirituality. The spirituality reflected in this publication is rooted in the Christian Scriptures and in the Catholic Social Thought tradition.

Christianity is a call to care for all of creation – 'God saw everything that He had made and behold, it was very good' (Genesis 1:31). It recognises the dependence of all on a caring God who is always faithful. We understand the Christian way of life as a following of Jesus. It is a way of being and acting that promotes the development of all people and the whole person simultaneously and in solidarity (*Populorum Progressio*, n. 43). This development takes place in the context of family, community and the wider society. It is facilitated by right relationships and is impeded when these relationships are strained, broken or in short supply.

Jesus explained his mission in the words 'I have come so that they may have life and have it to the full' (John 10:10). People and indeed all of creation are to enjoy fullness of life. It is a life where there is compassion, forgiveness, justice, peace, harmony, friendship, fidelity and truth. It is lived in an environment where physical, emotional, mental, moral and spiritual development is encouraged and facilitated.

As followers of Jesus we are expected to be life bearers and to reduce the obstacles that stifle life. We are to be bearers of 'good news.' In this daunting responsibility we are helped greatly by the Christian Scriptures and the Catholic Social Thought tradition which show us the way. Jesus lived out his understanding of his mission. He had come to proclaim the Reign of God. It was to be a situation where 'the hungry are filled with good things' (Luke 1:53) and where the 'lowly' would be guaranteed their right to a part of the earth's resources. As is shown in his actions and words, Jesus recognised that the social order of his day did not facilitate the development of all people. He advocated change and challenged those with power to bring about this change. He engaged with the social structures of his day. He named areas of oppression and challenged the leadership to live up to the ideals of their calling.

For the past two thousand years the followers of Jesus have promoted fullness of life and sought to bring this good news to all people but especially to poor and excluded people. Each generation, as affirmed by the Second Vatican Council has responded 'to the duty of scrutinising the signs of the times and of interpreting them in the light of the Gospel' (*Gaudium et Spes*, 4).

The Catholic Church through its large body of social teaching provides guidelines for Christian living. From Pope Leo XIII who called for major changes in the socio-economic order to the present day, the Church is calling us to transform society. Pope Paul VI has told us 'it is not enough…to point out injustice and to utter pious words and denunciation; such words lack meaning unless they are accompanied by responsible political and social action' (*Octogesima Adveniens*, n. 48). The Synod of Bishops in 1971 amplified this position in stating that '…participation in the transformation of the world fully appears to us as a constitutive dimension of the preaching of the Gospel' (*Justice in the World*, n.6).

We understand this to mean that we cannot claim to live by the Gospel unless we are engaged in the social reality of our time in a way that brings about transformation. Pope John Paul II continuing this theme called for a complete analysis to reveal unjust structures so that they may be examined and transformed to build a just earth (*Laborem Exercens*, 2). He also talked about the virtues needed to be involved in this transformation. 'To destroy such structures (of sin which impede the full realisation of those who are in any way oppressed by them) and replace them with more authentic forms of living in community is a task which demands courage and patience' (*Centesimus Annus*, 38). Recent social teaching alerts us not only to the structures that oppress people but also to the structures that cause destruction to the environment. Today the ecological crisis has assumed such proportion as to be the responsibility of everyone....there is an order in the universe which must be respected ... the ecological crisis is a moral issue' (Pope John Paul II, January 1, 1990). Social involvement is an intrinsic outcome of espousing Christian values. Engaging in activity to influence public policy and to generate structural change is answering the call to transform society which is a constitutive dimension of the Gospel.

For a Christian, social engagement involves reflection and action. It is about 'reading the signs of the times' to determine what is 'good news' for people today. We believe it involves a five step process

a)   Establishing the present social reality through research and dialogue.

b)   After reflection in the light of the Gospel highlighting the areas that need transformation.

c)   Articulating an alternative vision of society with specific targets for change.

d)   Prioritising the areas on which it is possible to work given the resources available.

e)   Devising action that will move society towards the targets identified and taking the required action.

Because the dominant culture tends to be a very comfortable one it is painful to critique it. It demands the ability to stand back from the *status quo* and view it through the lens of the Scriptures and Catholic Social Thought. Among the questions for the Christian community are the following: What supports the present generation of Christians in scrutinising the signs of the times? How can we be authentic in interpreting these signs in the light of the Gospel? What motivates and supports us in bringing good news to our brothers and sisters? This series of conferences with the subsequent publications is a contribution to the discussion of these questions.

This, the first of the series, is entitled *Spirituality and Poverty in a Land of Plenty*. We live in a country that has seen its prosperity grow dramatically over the past decade. Sustained economic growth has not delivered a fairer society. Despite our Christian tradition we have failed to distribute the prosperity so that there is nobody in need. Rather we have developed a deeply divided, two-tier society. Among the obstacles to enjoying the fullness of life are poverty, inequality and social exclusion.

The following pages address the questions of why poverty and social exclusion continue to be the norm for so many people in a society with a Christian background and where sufficient resources exist to tackle this issue effectively. They also look at what motivates and supports people who stay with the struggle of trying to change this situation. There are also many insights from the margins of society on how the issues might be addressed. This publication contains the three papers delivered at the conference. Conference participants who were seated at round tables were invited to share their insights and views after each paper. This sharing and initial responses from participants was recorded and edited and is included. For the benefit of readers who might like to do some personal reflection and/or engage in group discussion on this material study questions are added.

Brigid Reynolds, s.m.

Seán Healy, s.m.a.

Directors: CORI Justice Commission

1

Why Does Poverty Persist in a Land of Plenty?

EAMON O'SHEA AND BRENDAN KENNELLY

INTRODUCTION

This paper considers the current situation with respect to poverty and inequality in Ireland and imagines a future that has genuine equality of opportunity as a defining feature of both the economy and of society. The recent transformation of the Irish economy has been characterised as miraculous by some commentators and certainly the strong and unprecedented economic growth rates in recent years were not foreseen by anyone. Economic growth has yielded significant gains in respect of income and employment for many people in this country. Unfortunately, social gains have not been anywhere near as miraculous as the economic gains and the related issues of fairness and equality continue to be a problem for Irish society.

The successes and failures of the Irish economy, particularly with respect to poverty and income inequality, have been well-documented and it is not the intention of this paper to provide a comprehensive account of all that has happened in the recent decades (See Whelan *et al*, 2003; Nolan, 2003 and CORI, 2004).[1] However, some audit is required to provide a perspective on relative gains and losses and to document the persistence of inequality in Irish society. In summary terms, the reduction in absolute deprivation levels in recent years as a result of rapid growth in real incomes and falling unemployment has brought

1. See pages 37-38 for details of works cited.

about significant improvement in the lives of low income households. On the other hand, Ireland continues to have a high rate of relative income poverty. Similarly, income inequality has, at best, remained stable in Ireland during the 1990s and Ireland continues to have one of the most unequal income distributions in the OECD. Inequalities in health and education continue to persist with large numbers of people supplementing public provision through private consumption in both of these sectors. Sustained economic progress has not been accompanied by a commitment to greater fairness in the distribution of resources. There are no shared values in respect of optimal levels of equality in this society. Individualism and consumerism are now powerful forces in Irish society.

The economy is now the primary focus of public policy. Society is increasingly defined in economic terms using efficiency-based criteria. Economic growth, employment and productivity are prioritised ahead of family, public services and community-based living. The current emphasis on spatial planning, housing, transport and infrastructure is driven more by economic concerns than by virtuous social planning. There is no concept of social progress, no model against which to make judgements on the impact of economic development on social objectives. It is no wonder, therefore, that long-term trends for social goods (health, education, taxation, social care, housing and pensions) continue to be based on a dual philosophy that is closer to Boston than Berlin in terms of the welfare state continuum. A basic level of welfare provision is provided universally. This is done partly on the basis of need and partly on the basis of rights. This basic level may then be topped up by private means and/or tax expenditures. The proportion of people buying private health insurance and private education services has continued to increase. Exit to private consumption not public voice characterises the behaviour of Irish taxpayers and citizens.

The absence of change suggests a culture of contentment, that, as a whole, people are relatively satisfied with the *status quo*. And yet there remains an underlying concern about things that have been lost, of promises unfulfilled, of some metaphysical or spiritual needs that cannot be reached by materialism. More than 200 years ago Adam Smith made the following observation which continues to resonate today: 'How selfish man be supposed, there are evidently some principles in his nature which interest him in the fortunes of others and render their happiness necessary to him though he derives nothing from it except the pleasure of seeing it' (Smith, 1976). What are these principles and how strong is the interest in the fortune of others among men and women in this country? Have we reached optimal levels of fairness and equality in this country? If we have not reached desired levels, how can we better articulate demands for greater fairness and equality and have them implemented by government? These are some of the issues addressed in this paper. Section 1 of the paper considers the evidence on winners and losers in the Irish society. Section 2 puts forward reasons why the situation is as it is. Section 3 outlines some recommendations for the future, including the development of a new National Fairness Strategy.

1. ECONOMIC INEQUALITY IN IRELAND

POVERTY

The National Anti-Poverty Strategy (NAPS) was launched in 1997 with the objective of achieving a designated reduction in poverty over the period from 1997 to 2007. The Strategy Statement set out its overall objective as follows: 'over the period 1997-2007, the National Anti-Poverty Strategy will aim at reducing the numbers who are consistently poor from 9 to 15 per cent to less than 5 to 10 per cent.' The definition of poverty agreed under NAPS was as follows: 'People are living in poverty if their income and resources (material, cultural and social) are so inadequate as to preclude them from having a standard of living which is regarded as acceptable by Irish society generally.' The definition referred to participation 'relative to the norm for other people in society'. Table 1 (*page 18*) presents the figures for the proportion of households experiencing relative income poverty who are also experiencing basic deprivation of one or more items (consistent poverty) for the period 1994-

2001. There has been a significant fall in the level of consistent poverty between 1994 and 2001 leading to many revisions of the original NAPS target. This is undoubtedly good news even if there are on-going concerns that the non-monetary deprivation indicators need to be adjusted to reflect changing expectations and perceptions about what constitutes necessities relative to the norm for people in society. Similarly, there is no evidence of any significant concentration of cumulative disadvantage among certain groups of people living in particular locations. Poverty and unemployment are dispersed across the country with no evidence of increasing concentration through good times or bad in recent decades.

Table 1   **Percentage of Households Below Proportions of Mean Income and Experiencing Basic Deprivation in 1994/ 1997/1998/2000/2001**

	1994	1997	1998	2000	2001
50 per cent line	9.0	6.7	6.0	4.5	4.1
60 per cent line	15.1	9.7	8.0	5.8	5.2

Source: Whelan *et al,* (2003: 38); Equivalence scale A (1.0/0.66/0.33)

Table 2 (*page 19*) shows that the percentage of individuals in relative poverty has generally increased between 1994 and 2001. Furthermore, the depth of income poverty has also increased over this period (Whelan *et al,* 2003: 13). In general, what we have experienced in recent years is the failure of social welfare transfers to keep pace with the high rate of growth of average incomes in the economy. Two countervailing tendencies have influenced relative poverty rates in recent decades. The composition of 'at risk' households has changed over time depending on the performance of the economy and the generosity of the social welfare system. The most recent evidence suggests that the high risk categories for poverty are households headed by people who are ill/disabled, households headed by unemployed people and households headed by people engaged in home duties. The failure of social transfers to keep pace with average incomes has also significantly increased the vulnerability of households headed by elderly people to relative poverty.

Table 2   Percentage of Persons Below Median Income Poverty
            Lines
            (Based on Income Averaged Across Individuals)

	1994	1997	1998	2000	2001
50 per cent median income line	6.0	8.6	9.9	12.0	12.9
60 per cent median income line	15.6	18.2	19.8	20.9	21.9
70 per cent median income line	26.7	29.0	26.9	28.1	29.3

Source: Whelan *et al*, (2003: 12); Equivalence scale A (1.0/0.66/0.33)

INCOME INEQUALITY

The standard measure of the level of inequality in a country is
the Gini Coefficient. The Gini Coefficient varies between 0 and
1 with higher values indicating higher levels of inequality. Table
3 (*page 20*) shows the Gini Coefficient for a number of OECD
countries. Income distribution in Ireland is among the more
unequal among OECD countries. There appears to have been
little change in income inequality during the economic boom
(Nolan, 2003). Between 1994 and 2000 the share of total
equivalised income going to the bottom decile of the income
distribution fell but there was no corresponding large-scale rise
in the share of income going to the top decile. Indeed on the
evidence of the Living in Ireland Survey, the share of income
going to the top ten per cent of persons actually fell slightly
(Nolan, 2003). However, it should be pointed out that the ratio
of the top ten per cent of the population to the bottom ten per
cent in terms of income did actually rise during the second half
of the 1990s from 7.3 to 7.6 (Table 4, *page 20*). In addition,
Garvey and Murphy calculated Consumer price Indexes for
different income deciles and found that the increase in the
Consumer Price Index between 1994 and 2000 was much
higher for the lower deciles (Garvey and Murphy, 2004). The
evidence presented here also remains very aggregate and the
top ten percent may contain a significant number of very rich

people who have gained significantly in recent years. Anecdotal evidence would suggest that there may be a very select core of very rich people in the top decile leading to a significant tail at the upper end of the income distribution in this country.

Table 3   Gini Coefficient (latest available year)

Country	Gini Coefficient
Belgium	0.25
Finland	0.25
Germany	0.25
Netherlands	0.25
Norway	0.25
Sweden	0.25
Denmark	0.26
Luxembourg	0.26
Austria	0.27
France	0.29
Canada	0.30
Australia	0.31
Ireland	0.33
Italy	0.33
UK	0.35
USA	0.37

Source: Luxembourg Income Study

(http://www.lisproject.org/keyfigures.htm)

Table 4   Ratio of Equivalised Disposable Income Received by Top Decile to Bottom Decile: 1994-2000 Based on Household Budget Survey

Decile Shares	1994	1999-2000
Share Top 10%	24.1	24.4
Share Bottom 10%	3.6	3.2
Ratio	7.3	7.6

Source: CORI (2004)

HEALTH INEQUALITIES

The international evidence on inequalities in health is compel-
ling. People who live in disadvantaged circumstances have
more illnesses, greater distress, more disability and shorter lives
than those who are more affluent (Kunst and Mackenbach,
1994; Benzeval et al., 1995). Health researchers in Ireland have
also documented the existence of the 'gradient' – the negative
relationship between mortality and socio-economic status
(Nolan, 1990; Balanda and Wilde, 2001). Differences in health
outcomes are not confined to extremes of rich and poor, but
are observed at each step of the socio-economic ladder for all
causes of death. For example, males in the unskilled manual
group have a standardised mortality ratio (SMR) for injury and
poisoning almost 4 times greater than males in the higher
professional category (O'Shea, 1997).

O'Shea (2003) analysed trends in years of potential life lost
(YPLL) for men aged 15-69 over the period 1981 to 1991 in
Ireland. Years of potential life lost captures the social gradient
in respect of deaths at younger ages. Men in the poorer socio-
economic groups have YPLL rates between 2 and 3 times
greater than those in the richer professional categories in each
of these years. Not only do people in lower socio-economic
groups have higher mortality rates but they also tend to die at
younger ages. The highest YPLL rates are to be found in the
unskilled manual group, semi-skilled manual workers and the
farm labourer and fishermen category. The use of YPLL as a
measure of premature mortality also points to the importance
of respiratory disease and injury and poisoning as the major
sources of health inequality in this country with 5- and 6-fold
differences between rich and poor. Lives lost prematurely from
these two causes of death are not randomly distributed across
the population but occur disproportionately amongst the poorer
sections of the community, albeit with some qualifications for
injury and poisoning in 1991. The social gradient in YPLL
between the lower manual group and the upper non-manual
group also widened between 1981 and 1991. Widening inequalities between social groups are particularly evident in
mortality from diseases of the circulatory system, digestive

diseases and injury and poisoning.

One of the most frequently expressed concerns about the Irish health care system is in relation to access of public patients to some acute hospital services. The growth in the proportion of the population with private health insurance is in part, a reflection of this concern. Nolan and Wiley (2000) found that 98.6 per cent of the insured gave 'being sure of getting in to hospital quickly when you need treatment' as a very important or quite important reason for them having such insurance. Data on waiting lists and waiting times for some procedures bear witness to the reality underlying such concern (Harkin, 2001) and this may partly explain the government's preoccupation with access to health services. This is part of an international concern with the emergence of market conditions in the health sector allowing higher socio-economic groups access to better health care, where health and social care are seen as traded goods as opposed to rights. Privatisation of public services tends to impact adversely and disproportionately on more vulnerable groups in society, particularly as more vocal and influential consumers exit the public sector leaving an impoverished public health service behind.

EDUCATION AND SOCIAL MOBILITY

Increased participation at both secondary and third level has been evident in Ireland since the 1970s. Impressive completion rates to the end of second level with some 82 per cent of the cohort completing senior cycle programmes in 2002 reflect the emphasis laid on participation rates through the period 1970-95. However, such figures can also conceal several dimensions of educational disadvantage at each level of the education system leading Nolan et al (2000) to conclude that there was little evidence of a reduction in educational inequalities by social class in recent decades. Completion rates while impressive overall continue to be strongly influenced by socio-economic background with over one third of students from unskilled social class failing to complete the leaving certificate in 1997/98 (McCoy and Smith, 2004). An analysis of changes in class structure between 1973 and 1994 found that while many children of working class origin took advantage of increased educational opportunities, this did not come at the expense of a reduction in access to third level education for children of the professional and managerial class (Layte and Whelan, 2001, 105). The use of private grind schools by those who can afford to pay serves to exacerbate differences in educational performance by socio-economic group at second-level. Home address, school location, access to top-up grind schools and pupil socio-economic background remain critical in terms of educational outcomes and expectations (Clancy, 2002). This is true for all schooling because the degree of educational disadvantage at primary level impinges on future educational achievement and outcomes.

The relative disparity between tertiary and primary expenditure per student is higher in Ireland than in most other OECD countries, despite the well documented social returns to investment in primary education. Almost twice as much is spent on each student attending a third level institution as is spent on pupils in the primary sector (McCoy and Smyth, 2004). The disparity in spending between the primary and third-level sectors does little to promote educational advantage. Similarly, the exchequer invests 2.5 times more money per capita in the education of those who complete three years of third-level education than it does for those who leave school before the completion of post-primary education. Over time education has become a less important predictor of class attainment (Layte and Whelan, 2001, 101). One possibility is that employers may be relying more on class than educational achievements in situations where more applicants present with the same level of educational achievement. Interestingly, there is also evidence that property inheritance continues to play a strong role in determining class outcomes.

SECTION 2: UNDERSTANDING THE SITUATION

In this section we present a number of different frameworks that might help us understand the broad picture of economic inequality that we have outlined in the previous section. These frameworks are not meant to be competing against each other to come up with a single explanation for the current level of economic inequality. Rather, the point is that we need to think about this complex issue in a variety of ways if we are to bring about change (if indeed change is desired and/or possible).

The first possibility is that the level of economic inequality reflects the theory of social valuation that forms the basis for policy-making in Ireland. A theory of social valuation may either be explicitly articulated by policy makers though it is more likely that we can only try to discover the appropriate theory of social valuation by looking at policy choices and economic outcomes. It is also unlikely that any country will follow one particular theory of social valuation in all policy areas. To set up the discussion on which theory of social valuation is relevant in Ireland, it is useful to begin with two theories that strongly contrast with each other and see whether the contrast helps us to understand the current direction of public policy in Ireland. The two theories are market liberalism and democratic equality.

Market liberalism (which is related to theories such as neo-liberalism, neo-classical economics, or limited government) is based on strong versions of individualism. It argues that consumer sovereignty should be respected as much as possible, that individuals are the best judges of their own welfare (or wellbeing) and that they have every right to spend their money as they see fit. Market liberals tend to have a strong belief in individual rationality: people can anticipate their own futures better than others, such as the government. Outside the economic sphere, market liberals tend to be strong proponents of equality in areas such as political, legal and civil rights. In the economic sphere, market liberals tend to oppose redistribution for two reasons. One is that they argue that each person has the right to enjoy the fruits of his/her labour; the other is that they are wary of the disincentive effects of transfer programmes.

Democratic equality theory starts with the assumption (or presumption) that everyone is of equal value and so should be treated the same. It guarantees all law-abiding citizens effective access to the social conditions of their freedom at all times (Anderson, 1999). It justifies the redistribution required to secure this guarantee by appealing to the obligations of citizens in a democratic state. Anderson recognizes the need to identify particular goods within the space of equality that are of special egalitarian concern. One possibility would be to focus on what John Rawls calls primary goods, goods that everyone is presumed to want, for example, liberty, powers, opportunities, income and wealth, and the social bases of self-respect. There is a strong emphasis on equality of opportunity in the Rawlsian approach to democratic equality theory. Daniels argues that every citizen has a contingent claim on the resources needed to preserve normal functioning, as a way of protecting fair equality of opportunity (Daniels, 1988). For example, health care can keep us functioning as close to normal as possible, thereby ensuring that everyone has as much opportunity as possible to live a normal life. Thus, health status is treated as determinant of the range of opportunities open to individuals.

Neither market liberalism nor democratic equality fully captures the model of social valuation at work in Ireland. Instead, it may be that a hybrid theory, which we have called democratic inequality, captures the essence of public policy making in Ireland regarding income redistribution and the welfare state. There is a basic level of benefits available to everybody. These benefits are available partly on the basis of need and partly on the basis of rights. The level of benefits is high enough to mean that consistent poverty has been reduced to low levels, but not so high as to make much of an impact on relative poverty. Above the basic level of benefits lies a second tier which includes tax expenditures for pensions, social care and health and subsidies for education and health care (For further discussion see O Riain and O'Connell, 2000). The nature of the Irish welfare state as a mainly residual one is enhanced by the tendency of key decision-makers to think of equity issues as secondary to the overriding pursuit of efficiency. This tendency has continued during the era of social partnership. In particular, the Department of Finance continues to act on the basis that its primary role is to control expenditure instead of thinking about social objectives that can only be satisfied through increased expenditure.

The second explanation is that maybe the outcome regarding economic inequality reflects the preferences of individuals regarding redistribution. One possibility is that the level of economic inequality is chosen so as to maximize economic growth. Theoretically speaking, there are grounds for thinking that economic inequality could have either a positive or a negative effect on economic growth. A more unequal income distribution might be good for growth if it means that savings and hence investment will be higher. Also, a more unequal income distribution might increase the incentives for individuals to invest in human capital. On the other hand, a more unequal income distribution might mean that more people will be unable to borrow to make productive investments. Also, a more unequal income distribution may lead to greater social and political unrest which will discourage investment (See Kenworthy (2003) and the references therein for more discussion on these points).

Economists have devoted a great deal of attention to the relationship between inequality, social protection expenditure and economic growth in recent years. Sceptics will not be surprised to learn that few definitive conclusions have been reached or that different authors have reached very different conclusions. A recent paper by the OECD found no evidence that the level of income inequality affects GDP one way or another (Arjona *et al.*, 2002). Kenworthy (2003) reached a similar conclusion regarding the relationship between economic growth and income inequality. His preferred empirical results are that inequality had no effect on the cross-country variation in growth in the 1980s and 1990s. Arjona *et al* also found that higher social protection expenditure reduces output, though the effect was not large. By contrast, Lindert finds no statistical evidence that high levels of social transfers reduce economic growth (Lindert, 2004).

The past few years have seen a great deal of interesting work that tries to analyse the effects of different preferences for equality and beliefs about fairness on the level and nature of redistribution (Alesina *et al*, 2001; Alesina and Angeletos, 2003; Benabou and Tirole, 2002). Preferences for equality refer to preferences regarding the outcome of the socio-economic system with regard to variables such as income, health or education. Beliefs about fairness refer to beliefs that people hold regarding the fairness of the process whereby income, health and education are achieved. An important concept that is receiving a lot of attention is what effect the prospect of upward mobility might have on the likelihood that individuals below the median income would vote for more redistribution. This research suggests that attitudes with respect to the sources of wealth or poverty play a major role in explaining differences in the extent of redistribution. If people generally believe that incomes are earned in a fair way and that there is a reasonable chance of they moving up the income distribution then they will favour relatively low taxes and low redistribution. An important aspect of this issue is that individuals do not think simply of their current situation when asked about preferring higher levels of redistribution. They are likely to also consider their aspirations (both for themselves and their children). Indeed, it is possible that people might adopt aspirations that are unlikely to be realized in an effort to impose self control.

Some comparative evidence on attitudes has been collected by the World Values Survey. It suggests large differences between Americans and Europeans. The percentages in the Table 5 refer to those answering 'yes' to each question.

Unfortunately Ireland was not included in the 1994/5 wave

Table 5: Attitudes about poverty and fairness

	U.S.	Europe	Ireland
Are the poor trapped in poverty?	29%	60%	n.a.
Does luck determine income?	30%	54%	47%
Are the poor lazy?	60%	26%	n.a.

Source: Alesina and Angeletos (2003)

of the World Values Survey when the questions about the nature of poverty were asked. The question on whether income is earned by hard work or luck was asked in 1990/91 and the results indicate that at least at that time Irish people thought more like their fellow Europeans than like Americans. It would be surprising if some attitudes in Ireland to these issues had not been affected by the economic boom (though we are unaware of more recent surveys that might yield answers to some of these questions). Much of the political rhetoric would suggest that the number of people in Ireland who believe that there are plenty of opportunities for economic advancement and that it is people's personal responsibility to take advantage of them has grown in the past ten years. This may be true though there is a danger of believing rhetoric just because it is repeated often enough. At the very least, we need more research and thinking about these issues.

A third framework that might be useful for understanding why relatively unequal economic outcomes are realized in Ireland can be found in standard welfare state analysis. The European Commission uses Social Protection Expenditure (SPE) to measure the size of the welfare state. It includes all public social expenditures apart from education and the share of national income spent on social protection is widely used in the EU as a measure of welfare state effort. The most recently available data is for 2001 (Eurostat, 2004). It shows that SPE/GDP in Ireland has fallen from 20.3% in 1992 to 14.6% in 2001. This ratio is by far the lowest of all the EU countries, a point that remains true if you use the more appropriate SPE/GNP ratio for Ireland (which was 17.4% in 2001). On the other hand, SPE per capita has increased much more in Ireland than in the EU as a whole between 1992 and 2001. The increase in SPE per capita was 51.1% in Ireland compared to 18.5% in the EU as a whole. Despite this, SPE per capita in Ireland was only 60% of SPE per capita in the EU15 in 2000. By contrast, GNP per capita in Ireland was 98.8% of GDP per capita in the EU in 2001.

It should be noted that these figures are gross and don't take into account taxes that are paid on benefits or tax expenditures regarding social protection items such as health or pensions.

The OECD has published data on net social expenditure for selected countries for 1999. In most countries net expenditure is lower than gross expenditure. Direct taxes on social transfers are around 4% of GDP in Denmark, Sweden and the Netherlands but they are quite small in Ireland. The ranking of some EU countries in welfare state effort is changed when net rather than gross social expenditure is used. For example, net social expenditure is a lower percentage of GDP in the Netherlands or Denmark than in the UK. Ireland has the lowest welfare state effort when net social expenditure is used though the gap between it and other countries is smaller (European Commission, 2002, 15-16).

It is interesting to note that most of the difference between Ireland and the EU is due to differences in expenditures on elderly people and people with disabilities. In 1999, almost 80% of the difference between Ireland and the EU average regarding the SPE/GDP ratio was due to the difference between Ireland and the EU regarding expenditure on old age and survivors and expenditure on disability programmes. Expenditure on these categories was equal to 4.2 per cent of GDP in Ireland while expenditure on these programmes was equal to 14.3 per cent of GDP in the EU as a whole. Indeed, the share of national income being spent in all the other categories of social protection was just one and a half percentage points lower in Ireland than in the EU as a whole in 1999 (once account is taken of the difference between GDP and GNP in Ireland). Some of this gap can be explained by differences in the population structure. The old age dependency ratio (defined as the number of people aged 60+ divided by the number of people aged between 20 and 59) was 28% in Ireland in 2000. This was the lowest ratio in the EU and compares to an EU average of 39%. When account is taken of the age structure, the increase in expenditure in Ireland on old age pensions between 1991 and 2000 was 11% compared to 18% for the EU as a whole. Other indicators of the generosity of the benefits spent on elderly people in Ireland confirm that the level of benefits is low relative to average income in Ireland. The risk of falling under the relative poverty lines has increased for elderly people, especially women, in the 1990s

The European Commission have used different waves of the ECHP survey to assess how effective social protection systems are in reducing poverty. Using 1993 data it found that the Gini coefficient in Ireland was reduced from .553 to .333 by social transfers. Before transfers 42 per cent of households had less than half average income while after transfers 21.2 per cent were. Using 1995 data it found that individuals in the first quintile of the income distribution received 56 per cent of total transfers (other than pensions). Almost everyone (98%) in the first quintile received some social transfer and in all social transfers accounted for 81 per cent of total income of the first quintile. This last figure was much higher than the EU average and reflects the heavy reliance on means tested payments in Ireland (European Commission, 1998).

SECTION 3: COMMITTING TO EQUALITY

The picture presented in this paper is of a society that contains significant levels of inequality. Ireland has relatively high income inequality compared to other European countries. Inequalities exist and persist in both health and education, despite recent increases in public spending in both of these sectors. Economic growth has raised incomes for almost all but has not always impacted positively on the quality of life of citizens. The dominant ideology in the country is one of consumerism, with the emphasis on acquisition, accumulation and appropriation. There is a Darwinian game being played out where to get ahead someone else must lose and losing, even a little, can put you out of the game. And the losers are the weakest to begin with: those without education, those in poor health, those without a job, those without income or wealth.

There remains a residual concern for the poorest in society thereby ensuring that basic needs are met through social protection measures and public provision of education, housing and health care. But there seems to be strict limits to our egalitarian impulses and the values of fairness and justice are not often evident in public discussions on the allocation and distribution of resources. Social partnership, for example, may have delivered wage restraint and tax cuts for the productive economy but it has not provided the framework for a fundamental shift in attitudes to fairness and justice in the country. At the level of public discourse there is a conflict between the idea of continuous economic growth and certain prerequisites of human existence such as ethics and fairness. We seem to have forgotten what human beings need in order to flourish and grow.

And yet at an individual level all of us are capable of heroic acts of decency and kindness to people who are less fortunate. We are all capable of recognizing and acting upon higher order needs within ourselves to help others. People are able to reconcile their quest for personal freedom with their need for social solidarity. Similarly, most of us recognise the importance of fraternity, love, belonging, dignity and respect in our own lives and the problems that arise when any or all of these elements are absent. So why do we not seem able to understand the importance of a more active and sustained public policy to reduce inequalities in this country? Why in the face of persistent inequality with respect to income, health and education do we not demand redistributive programmes to eliminate these inequalities, whatever the cost? What needs to be done to translate individual concern about inequality into public action?

The first step in addressing persistent inequality is to find out how people generally perceive inequality in this country. We have already seen that it is possible that the current level of inequality is optimal for Ireland, as perceived by the majority of citizens. It may be that people want some minimum level of protection to be available to all but beyond that everything is possible: the prevailing distribution of income or the way opportunities are arranged and aligned is of no concern. As long as people believe that they can improve their own position then they are not concerned about how far away they are from the top income bracket in society. And it is possible for the majority of the middle classes to believe that they or their offspring can gain entry to at least the top quintile of the income distribution. Therefore, rather than wanting Ireland to become more equal, to look more like the Scandinavian countries, it is more fruitful to accept the prevailing income distribution in revealed preference terms. You may not like it but this is what it is.

The above analysis assumes perfect information. It may not be correct to assume that people know the true extent of income inequality in the country. The normal presentation of income distribution in terms of deciles or quintiles may be unhelpful in that regard. In cash terms, the 2000 Household Budget Survey reveals that the top 10 per cent of households receive an average weekly disposable income of €883, a sum that is eleven times greater than the €80 per week received by those households in the bottom decile. The capacity of these differences to shock is much less than if comparisons were made between the share of income going to the top 1 per cent of people and the bottom 1 per cent of people. We have never seen any published figures on the gains and losses at the very tail ends of the income distribution in recent years, but we suspect, given the extravagant salaries now paid to chief executives of large corporations and prominent superstars of media, business and sport that the distribution has widened by much more than is evident from decile comparisons. The question remains of course whether even with full knowledge about the extent of existing disparities in incomes and opportunities would people want to do something about them?   We cannot answer that question but it is likely that more information is better than less information when addressing the issue of the optimal level of inequality in society.

It is rare for people to be asked about their views on inequality. People are often asked about quality of life issues but rarely are they asked about how other people's quality of life affects theirs. Nor are people asked about whether all inequalities are equally bad or whether some inequalities are worse than others. We have never had to seriously consider what we might be willing to pay to reduce currently observed inequalities or to demonstrate the strength of our preferences for various public policy interventions to reduce inequality. For all the rhetoric about inequality and the linking of prosperity with fairness in various policy documents the discussion on how much inequality should be tolerated in this society has been muted. The Combat Poverty Agency in their review of the last five Budgets concluded that they have benefited the rich more than the poor. The question that matters is whether this is acceptable to us as a society and more importantly how can we change it if it is not acceptable?

It would be naive to count on the Irish political system to provide the leadership in respect of any debate on egalitarianism in Irish society. The political system in Ireland is not configured in such a way as to allow debate about efficiency/equity trade-offs in public policy. Moreover, the impact on the tax system is likely to be deemed too high a political price to pay for eliminating inequalities by any of the main political parties. Similarly, the egalitarian instincts of the ruling intellectual elite are generally weak and cannot be relied upon to promote policies that reduce inequalities. Indeed, some people in positions of influence in setting the agenda for public policy may regard inequality as a necessary prerequisite for an efficient market economy. That does not mean that the desire to address inequalities is absent in Irish society. Rather it is that no mechanisms have been found to link individual preferences for action on inequalities to public policy. This is why individuals and community groups have an obligation to instigate a national values debate which would address the question of where we stand on egalitarian issues. It may be that we ultimately agree that existing levels of inequality are what we want but at least that would be an advance on the current *ad hoc* and covert acceptance of distributional policies.

One way of addressing this issue would be to develop a National Fairness Strategy which would incorporate a values forum and public consultation process, leading ultimately to the setting of social norms and policy targets for equity across a number of different sectors and government departments. Lionel Jospin famously argued for a 'market economy not market society' on the basis that markets are value free, having great momentum but no sense of direction. A National Fairness Strategy could provide the direction for public policy that is needed to address inequality issues in Irish society. It could certainly address fundamental questions on the nature and direction of this society and whether the juxtaposition of economy and society has led to an improvement in quality of life and wellbeing for all citizens and not just for a privileged few. Philosophical consideration could be given to optimal levels of economic growth, the nature of social progress and meaning of solidarity between rich and poor and between generations. The new Strategy would have a number of potential social dimensions, including:

- Equality of opportunity as the central tenet of public policy programmes
- The elimination of poverty
- The reduction of income inequality
- Social inclusion and solidarity – not just in terms of money but in relation to employment, education, health, pensions and housing.

A National Fairness Strategy could have a major influence on health inequalities. At present, the goal of equal access to health care for equal need is the main strategy for reducing health inequalities in Ireland. This equity target has developed in response to legitimate complaints made against the existing system about the influence of private health insurance on access to health care in Ireland. However, the target of equal access for equal need reflects a lack of coherent thinking on the topic of equity and inequalities in health. Inequalities in health are strongly influenced by structural inequalities in society. In order to address health inequalities, there is an obligation on government to fundamentally and radically address the underlying structural inequalities which give rise to them. This means a serious investment in tackling poverty and reducing income inequality, social exclusion and the marginalisation of individuals and communities. A National Fairness Strategy would facilitate a new model of health production in Ireland, where the emphasis would be on the resources available to people to obtain higher levels health as much as on access to health care once illness occurs.

The pay-related nature of the welfare state is likely to influence attitudes to equality and inequality in Ireland. The availability of additional income from occupational pensions is bound to dilute concern about the adequacy of public pensions. Similarly, membership of private health insurance schemes reduces the likelihood of members experiencing poor or inadequate health care or having to wait a long time for treatment. The likely consequence of exposure to private medicine is that concern for the public health system is going to be reduced. Likewise, the availability of private fee-paying schools and the increasing emphasis on private tuition in the form of grind schools is likely to undermine commitment to public education and the elimination of social class inequalities with respect to completion rates and access to third-level education. Put bluntly, if people cannot see inequality, cannot touch disadvantage, cannot hear discrimination, then it is less likely they will be moved to reduce inequality, end disadvantage or eliminate discrimination. The absence of universality has a corrosive effect on equality that has not always been appreciated but which is real nonetheless. Conversely, the positive effect on equality of a new National Fairness Strategy incorporating universality and agreed social norms for the availability and utilisation of public goods cannot be overstated.

One of the main arguments against universality is, of course, the cost involved in the form of higher taxation. There are legitimate concerns about the negative impact of higher taxation on economic growth, competitiveness and employment in this country. There are, however, plenty of examples of high taxation countries that have prioritised public services ahead of private consumption and managed to achieve satisfactory levels of economic growth. You cannot have a fair society without having an adequate and fair taxation system. The debate about taxation has centred on the need to have low marginal tax rates to stimulate maximum economic effort, which will in turn lead to higher output in the economy, with claim and counter-claim as to the optimal rate. What is said less often is the role of taxation in providing the resources to achieve a more egalitarian society. This is a debate worth having, particularly since there is also good evidence that the tax system, through a combination of reliefs, allowances, exemptions and deductibles, is neither adequate nor equitable. Taxes as a proportion of income increase from low to middle incomes but tend to fall away rapidly at the very highest incomes. For example, the Revenue Commissioners estimate that 17 per cent of people with annual incomes over €250,000 pay tax at an effective rate of 20 per cent or less. Higher and more equitable taxation are necessary, if not sufficient conditions, for improved public services and a more equitable society.

CONCLUSION

This is a critical time for Irish society. Sustained economic growth has not delivered a fairer society. For years we were told to wait for the economic recovery that would lift all boats. The economic recovery came and delivered jobs and higher incomes but it has not led to a more just society. Significant inequalities continue to exist with respect to income, wealth, health and education. We need a National Fairness Strategy to address these inequalities. The need for a discrete and seismic change of direction has been recognized at various stages in the past in this society. The publication in 1958 of Economic Development and the subsequent First Programme for Economic Expansion created the conditions for a new and sustained type of industrial economy in Ireland. The publication of the Programme for National Recovery in 1987 provided the impetus for a new form of social partnership that continues to impact on economic and social progress in this country. A new National Fairness Strategy, incorporating a values framework and significant public consultation would now provide the basis for a sustained attack on inequalities in the coming decades. At the very least, it would tell us something more about ourselves.

REFERENCES

Alesina A. and G. M. Angeletos (2003), "Fairness and Redistribution: U.S. versus Europe", *NBER* Working Paper, No. 9502.

Alesina, A., E. Glaeser and B. Sacardote (2001), "Why doesn't the US have a European-style Welfare State?", *NBER* Working Paper, No. 8524.

Anderson, E. (1999), "What is the Point of Equality?" *Ethics*, Vol. 109, pp. 287-337.

Arjona, R., M. Ladaique and M. Pearson (2002), "Social Protection and Growth", *OECD Economic Studies*, No. 35, pp. 8-45.

Balanda, K. and J. Wilde (2001), *Inequalities in Mortality 1989-1998: A Report on All-Ireland Mortality Data*. Dublin: The Institute of Public Health in Ireland.

Benabou R. and J. Tirole (2002), "Belief in a Just World and Redistributive Policies", *mime, Department of Economics, Princeton University*.

Benzeval, M., Judge, K. and Whitehead, W. (1995), "Introduction" in M. Benzeval, K. Judge and W. Whitehead (eds.) *Tackling Inequalities in Health: An Agenda for Action*. London: King's Fund.

Daniels, N. (1988), *Am I my Brother's Keeper?* Oxford: University Press.

European Commission (1998), *Social Protection in Europe 1997*. Luxembourg: Official Publications of the European Community.

European Commission (2002), *Social Protection in Europe 2001*. Luxembourg: Official Publications of the European Community.

Eurostat (2004), "Social Protection in Europe," *Statistics in Focus: Population and social conditions* 2004 (6).

Garvey, E. and E. Murphy (2004), "A Consumer Price Index for Low-Income Households", *mimeo, Department of Economics, NUI, Galway*

Harkin, A.M. (2001). *Equity of Access to Health Services: Some Relevant Issues in an Irish Context*. Dublin: The Institute of Public Health in Ireland.

Kenworthy, L. (2003), "An Equality-Growth Tradeoff?", *Luxembourg Income Study*, Working Paper No. 362.

Kunst, A. and Mackenbach, J (1994), *Measuring Socio-Economic Inequalities in Health*. Copenhagen: World Health Organization,

Layte, R. and C. Whelan (2000), "The Rising Tide and Equality of Opportunity: The Changing Class Structure", pp. 90-108 pp. 310-339 in B. Nolan, P. O'Connell and C. Whelan eds. *Bust to Boom? The Irish Experience of Growth and Inequality*. Dublin: Institute of Public Administration.

Lindert, P. (2004), *Social Spending and Economic Growth*. Cambridge: University Press.

McCoy, S., and E.Smyth. (2003), "Educational Expenditures: Implications for Equality", pp. 65-97 in T. Callan, A. Doris and D. McCoy eds. *Budget Perspectives 2004*. Dublin: Economic and Social Research Institute.

Nolan, B., P. O'Connell and C. Whelan (2000), "Conclusion: The Irish Experience of Growth and Inequality", pp. 340-353 in B. Nolan, P. O'Connell and C. Whelan eds. *Bust to Boom? The Irish Experience of Growth and Inequality*. Dublin: Institute of Public Administration.

Nolan, B. (1990), "Socio-Economic Mortality Differentials in Ireland", *Economic and Social Review*, Vol. 21, No. 2, pp 193-208.

Nolan, B. (2003), "Income Inequality during Ireland's Boom", *Studies*, Vol. 92, No. 366, pp. 132-142.

Nolan, B. and M. Wiley (2000), *Private practice in Irish public hospitals*. Dublin: Economic and Social Research Institute.

O Riain S. and P. O'Connell (2000), "The role of the state in growth and welfare", pp. 310-339 in B. Nolan, P. O'Connell and C. Whelan eds. *Bust to Boom? The Irish Experience of Growth and Inequality*. Dublin: Institute of Public Administration.

O'Shea, E. (1997), "Male Mortality Differentials by Socio-Economic Group in Ireland", *Social Science and Medicine*, Vol. 45, No. 6, pp 803-809.

O'Shea, E. (2003), "Social Gradients in Years of Potential Life Lost in Ireland", *European Journal of Public Health*, Vol. 13, pp 327-333.

Smith, A. (1976), *The Theory of Moral Sentiments*. Oxford: University Press.

Whelan, C., R. Layte, B. Maitre, B. Gannon, B. Nolan, D. Watson and J. Williams (2003), *Monitoring Poverty Trends in Ireland: Results from the 2001 Living in Ireland Survey*, Dublin: The Economic and Social Research Institute.

Participants' Responses

CAROL DORGAN LSA [Ed.]

The participants, on arrival, found themselves already assigned to one of twelve round table groups in the large Conference Room, tables seating approximately ten people, all with previously briefed facilitators. Following each presentation the groups had 45 minutes to answer certain questions, chosen to elicit comprehensive responses, which were recorded on Flip Charts by the Facilitators. There was no doubting the engagement of everyone in this process, and the questions were designed to find actions appropriate to the perceived insights.

The process used by the round tables following the first two presentations was as follows :

1. Invite participants to share an insight that has personal implications for them

2. Brainstorm involving all participants, What are the key insights/ideas that are calling for a response

3. Participants identify two priorities from the material recorded on the flip chart.

4. Concentrate on the two insight ideas which are the most frequently identified as priorities. Participants are invited to name the actions which would promote these insights/ideas. These are then recorded on flip chart.

What follows is a summary of what groups said. I have concentrated on only two questions put to the groups – Questions 2 and 4 above – as they seem to contain all else that was said.

KEY INSIGHTS CALLING FOR A RESPONSE

The two speakers spoke of what they perceived as the prevailing values informing the Irish political system and Irish society as a whole, which allow increasing social inequality to continue largely unchallenged. This is a stark reminder of a national reality calling out for the transforming power of the Gospel. Political decisions reflect values. It was clear to everyone that these values need to be questioned, and many participants were taken by the proposal for a National Fairness Strategy as well as that of a national debate on values. Ireland, as one participant remarked, is more than 'an economy.' People must be central. They must not be sacrificed to economic efficiency. We need to educate ourselves and others to be critically aware of what is happening and not allow ourselves to be manipulated by media or by politicians at election times. In this respect, a strategy must be created to ensure that the voices at the 'grass roots' can be heard.

WHAT ACTIONS WOULD PROMOTE THESE INSIGHTS?

Since the majority of insights and ideas circled round the question of values and a National Fairness Strategy, it was to be expected that education would feature strongly as a form of action. Interesting questions were raised. Who and for what are we educating? What kind of values are being transmitted and by whom? Do we, adults as well as young people, need a better education – a 'conscientization'? [1] And how do those charged with policy and political decision-making become educated and conscientized? It was clear that this assembly felt strongly that the latter question was vital.

Ways to bring about this national awareness-raising were firstly, the use of the media, one group specifically mentioning the investigative *Prime Time* television programmes. Another vehicle suggested was the 'Active Citizenship Voter Education Programme' pioneered by the Vincentian Partnership for Jus-

---

1. 'Conscientization' is a term popularized by the Brazilian educator Paulo Freire to denote a process whereby adults, through a specific adult education process, become politically and socially aware of unjust structures affecting them and of ways to bring about change in a non-violent way.

tice[2], which continues to be a very successful way of educating and mobilizing local community groups in many parts of the country around the political process. Then there was the proposal to work with community and youth groups, training leaders to conduct meetings by means of the 'multiplier effect' – these leaders training others etc. – so that the entire country, including its educational institutions, is focused on values at election times. The CORI Justice Commission was seen as an extremely valuable and credible resource which might initiate a Forum on Values

A voice that is not sufficiently heard in the halls of Dáil Éireann or the offices of Civil Servants when social policy is being devised and debated, is the voice of those 'on the margins' of Irish society. Such voices, groups insisted, must be heard and brought into the process. The Social Partnership process initiated some years ago by the Government has the potential to ensure a much greater inclusion of marginalized groups in the political process and in the fruits of social policy decisions.

2. The Vincentian Partnership for Justice: a group of people representing the Society of St. Vincent de Paul, the Vincentian Congregation and the Daughters of Charity. It was established in 1996 to tackle poverty and exclusion by working for social and economic change. It can be found at Ozanam House, 53 Mountjoy Square, Dublin 1..

Study Questions

If you wish to give more time to reflect on the issues raised in this paper the following questions may help you. They are also intended to help group discussion on the topic. As a preparation for group discussion participants are encouraged to reflect on the questions privately.

Feedback and comments are welcome by the CORI Justice Commission, Bloomfield Avenue, Donnybrook, Dublin 4.

Why Does Poverty Persist in a Land of Plenty?

'This chapter considers the current situation with respect to poverty and inequality in Ireland and imagines a future that has genuine equality of opportunity as a defining feature of both the economy and of society.'

1. What do you see as some of the manifestations of the present poverty and inequality?

2. What are the underlying causes of the high rate of income poverty in Ireland to-day?

3. What can we do to counteract the "focus on economic growth, employment and productivity at the expense of family, justice services and community based living"?

4. Identify 4/5 key elements which you believe should be included in the development of a National Fairness Strategy

5. Envision an Ireland in which a National Fairness Strategy is in the process of implementation and identify for yourself a role in this implementation.

2

Spirituality from the Margins

TIMOTHY RADCLIFFE OP

When you are invited to give a lecture, the organisers have to know the title long before you have even vaguely begun to think about what you wish to talk. And so when Tom Jordan contacted me a few months ago, I blithely suggested the title, 'A spirituality from the margins.' It seemed a nice idea at the time.

It was only when, much later, I sat down to try to prepare the lecture that I realised what a stupid topic I had chosen since I am almost as unmarginal as it is possible to be. The only time when I have had the briefest glimpse of what it might be to be on the margins was when I was a University chaplain in London. We went out every Monday on the soup run. And at the final point of distribution, it was the custom to stop for half an hour to share in the soup drinking. I was quietly parked on a bench chatting with two people, when another charity – which shall be nameless – turned up. When they offered me a cup of soup, I politely declined. It was notoriously disgusting. And this young man from the charity gave me a lecture, saying that as I was down and out, then I must not be too proud to accept charity when I needed it. This gained me a lot of street cred!

I am reminded of the Bishop of Lincoln, who when he was Bishop of Dover, got into an empty railway carriage. Soon it filled up with people on a day out from a mental hospital. Someone in charge came to count that they were all there. 'One, two, three, four', he said including the Bishop. 'Actually I am the Bishop of Dover'. 'Yeah, OK, five, six, seven.'

As a University educated white male, I am already from the

centre of society. And I will not embarrass you or myself by saying just how establishment is my own background. In fact my greatest claim to fame is that I was described by Terry Eagleton in a novel as washing up in the priory 'with a jovial air, like royalty driving a steam engine.'[1] The only slight element of liminality in my youth was the fact of being Catholic, but nowadays even Catholics are more or less accepted in England.

When I was Master of the Dominican Order I visited the margins. I spent a fair bit of time in war zones, such as Rwanda, Burundi, the Congo and Iraq. I went to leprosaria in Asia and Africa, innumerable Aids clinics, and I visited the poor and violent barrios of Latin America. But I was always only a visitor. I went to support my brethren and sisters who worked in these places. I have never lived in the margins. Maybe the subtitle for this lecture should be, to use the words of the Cistercian monk Thomas Merton, 'The Conjectures of a Guilty Bystander.' It would be presumptuous of me to try to articulate the wisdom and spirituality of the marginalized. They must speak and we must listen. All that I will do is to reflect a little on the different forms of marginalization that we encounter.

The first question that this Guilty Bystander would ask is this: if we are looking for a spirituality of the margins, then on the margins of what? Zymunt Bauman[2] has argued that our society is in the process of a deep transformation. We are moving out of a previous form of capitalism that is typified by Ford Motor Cars. In fact it is usually called Fordism. This was founded on the production of heavy goods, cars and steel and ships and so on, in industrial centres. The poor came to these centres to seek work, places like Belfast and Manchester. And the products were exported from these centres around the world. And this implied a strong mutual commitment of capital and labour. They fought great battles, but like a grumpy married couple, they remained wedded to each other. The workers needed salaries and the factories needed a trained and stable workforce. When Ford doubled the salaries of his workers it was because he

1. Terry Eagleton, *Saints and Scholars* London 1987 p.71

2. Zymunt Bauman, *Liquid Modernity*, Cambridge 2000, p. 122

had to keep them. So in this society it was clearer where were the margins. The marginalized where those who clustered around these centres, unemployed, or with no fixed contract or no expertise that gave them security. They were encamped around the walls of the city. It was a geography of centres: industrial centres, central cities and central countries.

But we are entering a new world, which Bauman calls 'Liquid Modernity.' And what zings around the World Wide Web are not so much heavy objects as signs and symbols, information, logos and brand names. These exchanges build up our global village. Of course you can argue that millions of people are marginalized here too. The vast majority of Africans do not have access to Internet. 65% of all human beings have never used a telephone, and 40% do not have electricity. And so one might say there are the marginalized who sit on the edges of our global village just as they did around the great industrial cities of our parents. Yet in a sense everyone does belong now. There are the bonds of the drug trade, of money laundering, the criminal mafias, prostitution, the diamond trade and the sale of body parts. No one escapes from those networks. Africa may be largely excluded from the networks of investment and legitimate trade, but the civil wars in places like the Congo and Angola tie them in with the sale of arms and diamonds and minerals.

The powerful people in this new world of Liquid Modernity are not those who are settled at the centre and who draw people to their factories to seek work. They are, Bauman says, the nomads, who can wander around the world at will. The old pact between capital and labour is broken. The rich are those who can quickly disengage and move on. Power is mobility. If wages become too high in Dublin, then production moves to Mexico.

So instead of contracts for life, one has short-term contracts, rolling contracts or no contracts at all. Bauman writes, 'Brief encounters replace lasting engagements. One does not plant a citrus tree to squeeze a lemon.'[3] I remember crossing the border from the USA into Mexico to visit our community in Mexicali.

3. *ibid*

There are hundreds of maquiladores, factories where workers have virtually no rights at all, producing for American Multinationals. If there is any fuss, then the Multinational will just get up and go.

Bauman writes, 'People who move and act faster, who come nearest to the momentariness of movement, are now the people who rule. And it is the people who cannot move as quickly, and more conspicuously yet the category of people who cannot at will leave their place at all, who are ruled. Domination consists in one's own capacity to escape, to disengage, to "be elsewhere", and the right to decide the speed with which all that is done – while simultaneously stripping the people on the dominated side of their ability to arrest or constrain their moves or to slow them down.'[4] In fact many multinationals now do not bother to own solid things like factories. For Nike, it is enough to own the brand. Others can get on with the time consuming business of building sweatshops and employing people. That ties one down. Owning the idea and the name is enough if one wishes to be unencumbered. The nomad travels light.

Of course there are centres: New York, London and Tokyo are all centres. September 11th was a symbolic attack on the centres of American economic and military power. But the nomad, with his cell phone and laptop can be anywhere. And so governments must cooperate in the mobility of capital, knocking down the barriers and allowing free access. The true centres today are not of place or nation but in the information networks. As Lash and Urry wrote, we have moved 'from place to flow, from space to stream, from organized hierarchies to disorganization.'[5] Social structures have been replaced by information structures. The poor today are not so much the dispossessed as the disconnected.

So marginalization is complex. The metaphor is spatial, and the poor and powerless do suffer from exclusion from various spaces and places. But there are all sorts of other marginalizations. They are marginalized from networks of

4. *ibid.*, p.119

5. Scott Lash and John Urry, *Economies of Signs and Space* London 1994, p. 323

information and communication, disconnected. They are marginalized in the sense that governments resist their movement. They must stay put while the nomads move on. They are marginalized from decision-making process, from power. They are marginalized from the identity of the rich and powerful. So how can we as a Church respond to these complex and overlapping exclusions? How can we be a sign of the Kingdom in which all of humanity will belong?

The first form of marginalization from which the poor suffer is exclusion from the networks of information. Scott Lash and John Urry argue that in our world social structures have been partially replaced by information structures. To be at the centre is not spatial, but it is to have the power of access to knowledge. The rich above all own information rather than solid things like buildings and real estate. Just to take one example, crop seeds. Many of the poor of our planet depend upon the fertility of the land to survive. They struggle to live from the annual miracle of planting and harvesting. The rich do not need to take ownership of their land. They want to own the fertility of the seeds, as their intellectual property. About ten major companies are buying germ plasm. According to Jeremy Rifkin, they 'then slightly modify the seeds or strip out individual genetic traits, or recombine new genes into the seeds and secure patent protection over their "inventions." The goal is to control, in the form of intellectual property, the entire seed stock of the planet.'[6]

As a Church, we can react on two fronts. First of all there is the struggle to prevent the rich from taking possession of the fertility of the planet. It is not theirs or anyone's to own. There is the struggle of advocacy by bodies like Trócaire and CAFOD to resist this scandalous stealing of what is humanity's common possession. There are also the thousands ways in which the programmes of these agencies try to open the gates into the networks of information for the poor. The rich are the gatekeepers. We must go around opening the gates, springing the locks, handing over the passwords. In Brazil there have been some amazing results from teaching basic computer skills to

6. Jeremy Rifkin, *The Age of Access* London 2000 p.66

people from the poorest *barrios* of São Paulo. Once they have access to the net, they do astonishing things. Or think of Chiapas in Mexico. The guerrillas have used the World Wide Web brilliantly in their resistance to the government. Some mysterious reason, as I discovered during my visit to Mexico, the government is convinced that the Dominicans are behind it all! I was followed by secret police for three weeks and interrogated by the Prime Minister at length!

But as a Church, we also offer this information society something else, which may ultimately be far more subversive, which is wisdom. Seventy years ago, T.S.Elliot wrote 'Where is the wisdom we have lost in knowledge? And where is the knowledge that we have lost in information?[6]' Today I wish to suggest how, faced with these multiple marginalizations, the Church offers a Eucharistic wisdom. This is a way of seeing and being that is in fundamental opposition to the exclusions of our society.

The World Wide Web is the heart of the information society. But we can use it, if we have the imagination, to spread something quite different, which is wisdom, the wisdom of the gospel and of the marginalized. In this lecture I want to make some simple suggestions as the nature of this wisdom by looking at how the Eucharist responds to various forms of marginalization.

The most fundamental marginalization of the poor is from power. I have no expertise in economics at all, but it is well established that most of the international institutions which are supposed to be at the service of overcoming poverty and building a fairer world, such as the WTO, WB and the IMF, are not run democratically. They are at the service of the interests of the rich nations. Structural adjustment loans are given on the condition that poor economies are open to exploitation by the rich. Noam Chomsky has shown that the United States is solely interested in the UN is so far as it can serve its own goal of global dominance. And you will know much more than I do about the exclusions from power suffered by the poor within Irish society.

7. T.S. Eliot, *The Rock*

What can our Eucharistic wisdom offer in response? What does it say about power?

The Last Supper was celebrated in the face of the clash of two sorts of power. There was the brutal power of the military and religious authorities, who were coming to arrest Jesus and kill him. And there was the power of Jesus, which was that of signs. The whole gospel of John is structured around his signs, from the wedding of Cana to the raising of Lazarus. This is a different sort of power. It is not magical. Jesus is not a first century Gandalf any more than St Peter is Frodo. Jesus' power lay in the meaning of what he did. His signs spoke God's word, which creates and recreates. It is a semiotic and sacramental power, which is the speaking of a word of truth.

As the soldiers draw near to arrest Jesus, the synoptic gospels tell us that he performed a sign, taking bread, breaking it and sharing it, saying 'This is my body, given for you.' On Good Friday, the clash of these two forms of power comes to a climax in the meeting of Jesus and Pilate. Pilate says to Jesus, 'Do you not know that I have the power to crucify you.' But Jesus relies on this different sort of power. He says to Pilate, 'I have come into the world to bear witness to the truth. Everyone who is of the truth hears my voice.' Pilate replies 'What is truth?' and notoriously does not stay for an answer. He does not need to. He has soldiers.

Two weeks ago we celebrated Easter. That is the vindication of the power of the man of signs over the dumb and brutal powers of this world. 'The light shines in the darkness, and the darkness has not overcome it.' Our Eucharistic wisdom is that the power of meaning and of truth is ultimately stronger than any brute force.

We live under an ever darker shadow of violence: September 11th, the war in Iraq, the bombs in Madrid, the violence in the Middle East. In the face of this brutality, which overwhelmed Jesus and put him on a cross, we ultimately can make signs which speak of peace and justice. That is more powerful than armies.

Let me share with you one small example. Some American Dominicans decided to commemorate the first anniversary of

9/11, by holding a month long fast of just water. There were brethren, sisters and a lay Dominican. Some others joined just for a short time, like myself,f or a couple of weeks. It is a good way to loose weight! As the threat of war developed, that became another focus. We all had T-shirts that said, 'There must be another way.' We camped in Union Square, just north of Ground Zero, and we spoke to hundreds of people every day who came to question us and read our pamphlets. Many Jews and Muslims came and joined us for prayers three times a day. What astonished me was the symbolic meaning of fasting was immediately understood, even by the young, except by the young man who came to eat this hamburger and French fries – sorry Freedom fries – with us every day, and which smelt ever more delicious. People understood this symbolic act. It spoke. And every day there were TV cameras and journalists to transmit it.

Now, admittedly it does not seem to have had much effect. There are no records of Bush phoning Blair to consider cancelling the war because the Dominicans were fasting in New York. I would suggest that it is through such a care for the meaning of what we say and do, then we open windows for God's transforming grace in the world. It is attentiveness to significance, and not brute force, that we share in God's speaking a word that brings the Kingdom, that says 'Let human beings flourish' and they will.

We believe that God works through small signs. For our God, the smaller the better. God had to get Gideon's army down from 30,000 people to 300 before he would let him thrash the Midianites. Jesus cured only a few blind people, and a few of the paralysed. God needs just a tiny window for his transforming grace to work, otherwise we might misunderstand the nature of his power. In *The Merchant of Venice* Portia says, 'How far that little candle throws his beams/So shines a good deed in a naughty word.' Whatever we do to the least of his brothers and sisters, we do to him. What signs can we make that speak the Kingdom now?

Let me share with you two little examples which touched me.

Recently I visited an Aids hospice in Phnom Penh, run by an American priest, Jim. Jim is not a spring chicken, and he is struggling to learn Khmer. I have been to Aids hospices all over the world, but I have never seen such emaciated figures. Some of them get back enough strength to go back to their families for a little while. Most of them come there to die. I watched one utterly skeletal figure of a young man, having his hair washed and cut, with a look of such utter peace on his face that I wept. And it would be easy to wonder what difference all this will make to the course of history. A few people live a little longer and then die in dignity. It is a tiny speaking of the Word, 'Let human beings flourish', and we will.

Another one: The most moving Christmas vigil that I have ever attended was in Paris in 1995. It was the Christmas Mass for the tramps, celebrated in a big tent in the centre of Paris. The priest was a Spanish Dominican, Pedro Meca, who lives like a tramp on the streets of Paris and comes back to his brethren just once a week for a shower and a big meal. I think that the brethren hope that he has the shower before the meal! All the destitute, the homeless, and the bums were invited. A thousand came. It was a celebration of intense if sometimes befuddled happiness. The altar was made of cardboard, to celebrate the Christ who was born for all those who live in cardboard boxes today. When Pedro pulled the cork of the wine bottle at the offertory, cheers rang out. Afterwards everyone was invited to a superb banquet. That was a sign of the Kingdom. That was a gesture that reached across the divisions of rich and poor and spoke of the joy of the Kingdom. So faced with margianlization from power, we can perform signs which speak God's powerful word.

So there's marginilization from information structures, marginalization from power structures. A third way in which we may marginalize people is by cutting them out from our identity. We excise them from any awareness of who we are as human beings. We make them disappear. The early explorers described much of the planet as *terra nullius*, empty land. There was no one there, that they could see. Raymond Gaiti has written a beautiful book called *A Common Humanity*. He writes,

'A Spanish song often quoted by Simone Weil, says, "If you want to become invisible, there is no surer way than to become poor." Weil goes on to say, "Love sees what is invisible."' [8] Black people are often invisible to white people, poor people to the rich, women to men. Or they are noticed, but as objects rather than subjects. They have identities which are given to them, rather than ones that they share in shaping. As Rowan Williams wrote, 'Only certain people have the right to construct an identity for themselves; others have their roles scripted for them.'[9] The poor have only walk on parts in the stories of the rich, and no ad-libbing is allowed. They may be marginal to our understanding of who we are. As Mary Daley said of women, 'The power of naming has been stolen from us.'

I have just returned four days ago from the USA. I was there for five days and I looked at several newspapers and the news on three of four TVs stations. There were lots of reports about death in Iraq, but the only people who appeared to die there were American soldiers. There was nothing about the death of Iraqi kids, killed by Coalition forces. They were consigned to invisibility!

Faced with this marginalization, the Last Supper has a wisdom. It is offered 'for you and for all.' It is the sacrament of the unity of all humanity. None of us will know fully who we are until the Kingdom. In his Las Casas lecture last December in Blackfriars, Oxford, Terry Eagleton said that global identity is an oxymoron, like Alabama *haute cuisine*! It cannot be articulated now. We can make signs that speak of it and thus help it come to be. What are the signs that may speak of our present incompleteness?

Of course the most important thing is to ensure that the marginalized make their own signs, unscripted and unexpected. But we too can do something. Raymund Gaita is an Australian philosopher who used to work in a mental hospital and he describes the effect on him of the visits of a nun. 'One day a nun came to the ward. In her middle years, only her

8. Raymond Gaiti, *A Common Humanity: Thinking about Love and Truth and Justice*, London 2000, p. xx.

9. Rowan Williams, *On Christian Theology* p. 280

vivacity made an impression on me until she talked to the patients. Then everything in her demeanour towards them – the way she spoke to them, her facial expressions the inflexions of her body – contrasted with and showed up the behaviour of those noble psychiatrists. She showed that they were, despite their best efforts, condescending, as I too had been. She thereby revealed that even such patients were, as the psychiatrists and I had sincerely and generously professed, the equals of those who wanted to help them; but she also revealed that in our hearts we did not believe this.'[10] She made the humanity of the mental patients visible. Her behaviour was revelatory.

When the war in Iraq was clearly on the way, the Dominican Family in the United States distributed bumper stickers saying 'We have family in Iraq.' Of course this referred in the first place to our Dominican sisters and brothers in Iraq. But it also was supposed to startle people into the realization that we have Muslim brothers and sisters in Iraq. We were planning to kill our own flesh, our kith and kin.

When I was Master, for some mysterious reason the brothers and sisters always gave me clothes. I was constantly returning to S Sabina with my bags stuffed with shirts and T-shirts. Many of these had Dominican logos and symbols of them. When the time came for me to leave Rome I took hundreds of these down in bags to the S Egidio distribution centre in Trastevere, where they could be given to the poor. I loved to imagine that the beggars on the streets of Rome are all clothed with shirts proclaiming their Dominican identity. Of course really I would also need T-shirts which proclaimed my identity with them! Of course our beloved Church is still disfigured by the effective exclusion of women from the centre of its life. This is obvious and shameful. What signs can we enact that will heal this wound at the heart of our communion?

So marginalization from information networks, from power structures, from our identity. Finally, even in our liquid and nomadic world, there is still spatial exclusion. We lock people out of our space. We lock people out of our countries. There has

10. Op.cit., p.18

never in human history been such vast movements of people. Like our ancestors, great tribes of people are moving west trying to settle in our lands. One of the most powerful images of this were the pictures of those holding centres in Calais, for the thousands of people who every day tried to get through the Channel Tunnel into England, climbing on trains, running through the dark, captured and trying again and again. But the gates are being ever more carefully guarded. In Holland the new government is beginning the process of expulsion. It looks as if Belgium may be next.

Inside our countries there are also new areas from which the poor are excluded. Increasingly in England – I do not know about Ireland – people live in gated communities. You must be invited inside otherwise the security guards will not let you pass. In America these are called 'Common Interest Developments' or CIDs. Jeremy Rifkin, writing at the end of the last century, reckoned that by the year two thousand there would be almost a quarter of a million CIDs in the States, with 48 million people living in them. There must be far more by now. They are safe havens in a world that is getting more violent. So wealth can buy you seclusion and safety from the wild people clambering on the outside.

In the face of this marginalization, what wisdom does the Eucharist offer? Our community is gathered around the altar in the memory of the one who was cast out. He is 'the stone which the builders rejected which has become the corner stone' (Ps. 119). As James Alison has written, 'God is among us as one cast out.'[11] At the centre of our worship is the one who was crucified outside the walls of the city. So the Eucharist invites us to make a home in which the dichotomy between centre and periphery is transcended. As it says in the Letter to the Hebrews, 'Therefore let us go forth to him outside the camp and bear the abuse he endured. For here we have no abiding city, but we seek the city which is to come.' (Heb 13:13).

A lawyer asks Jesus who is his neighbour. The parable of the Good Samaritan turns the question on its head. Jesus concludes by asking him, 'which one *made himself* neighbour to the man

11. James Alison, *Knowing Jesus* p.71

who fell among thieves?' (Luke 10:36). The parable works by moving from the centre which is Jerusalem to the periphery which is Jericho. It carries us from the holy world of the Temple, to the outside, the place of those unclean Samaritans. The new liturgy of holiness is enacted by the side of the road. Most fundamentally it carries us from that centre which is ourselves, asking who are our neighbours, to find ourselves centred on the man who has fallen among thieves. The parable snatches the rug of our narcissism from under our feet.

When Thomas Merton became a Catholic he wrote, 'Now I had entered into the everlasting movement of that gravitation which is the very life and spirit of God. God's own gravitation towards the depths of His own infinite nature. His goodness without end. And God, that centre Who is everywhere, and whose circumference is nowhere, finding me. And He called out to me from His own immense depths'. I was really struck by the words, 'that centre who is everywhere and whose circumference is nowhere', which I have just discovered are adapted from words of Allan of Lille.[12]

As William Cavanagh said, 'In Christ the dichotomy of centre and periphery is overcome.'[13] Jesus summoned us beyond a universe structured by sacred centres. As he said to the Samaritan woman, 'Woman, believe me, the hour is coming when neither on this mountain nor in Jerusalem will you worship the Father...The hour is coming, and now is, when the true worshippers will worship the Father in spirit and in truth' (Jn 4: 21,23)

This will obviously affect how we understand what it means to celebrate the Eucharist. Our Church structures – parish and dioceses – reflect an agricultural world of villages and market towns. We gathered in our natural community centres and most people could hardly imagine anything else. Already the world of the Industrial Revolution strained that model. But how can

12. Quoted by St Bonaventure, in *The Soul's Journey into God*, trans. Ewart Cousins, New York, 1978, p.100, c.f. William Cavanagh 'The city: Beyond secular parodies' in *Radical Orthodox7, ed. J Millbank, Catherine Pickstock and Graham Ward*, London 1999, p. 200

13. ibid, p.195.

we understand our Christian community in the world of Liquid Modernity? How may we gather in Christian communities which do not reflect the exclusions of this modern world and which point beyond the polarities of centre and periphery? If we do not, then our parishes will consecrate marginalization. Helder Camera, the Archbishop of Recife in Brazil, was often accused of being a communist because of his concern for the poor who live in the *favellas* on the hills around the city. He said, 'If I do not go up the hills into their *favellas* to greet them as my brothers and sisters, then they will come from the hills into the cities with flags and guns.'

An image that comes to mind is that of making bread. It is a traditional metaphor for the Christian community. In the Didaché, one of the oldest Christian documents after the New Testament, we can find it already: 'As this broken bread, once dispersed over the hills, was brought together and became one loaf, so may thy Church be brought together from the ends of the earth into thy kingdom.'[14] Now I must admit that I have never made bread. One of my ambitions for my sabbatical was that I would learn to do so, but time slipped by without a single loaf. But like a typical modern person, instead of doing it, I watched a TV programme about it. According to Jamie Oliver, the Naked Chef, instructing his 15 apprentices, it appears to involve constantly rolling out the dough and gathering it into the centre, and rolling it out again. Bread making involves a long process of bringing the margins into the centre and then spreading the centre out into the margins. This indeed was what the Naked Chef was doing himself, in gathering in 15 unemployed people into his kitchens and teaching them how to cook and then sending them out to start their own projects. And it may be in this interchange of centre and margin, this kneading of the dough, that we may be a community which images Christ in whom there is neither centre nor periphery.

We need to knea `d the bread of the Eucharist through this dynamism of exchange. So this involves a going out to the victim, to be one with them, and a gathering in so that he or she

14.   9.4 *Early Christian Writings,* trans. Maxwell Staniforth, London 1968 p..231

can be one with us. The typical outside is the leper. In the Philippines we have communities of Dominican laity who live and work with lepers. In fact many are themselves lepers. I remember how profoundly moving it was in Manila, at a gathering of the Dominican Family, to see these groups of lepers arrive to take their place in our community. But that is only half of the movement. Even more touching, in every sense, was the Christmas Day that I went to spend with them, to be welcomed in their community, to dance and sing in their home. Such reciprocities can be complex and sensitive. In the time of apartheid, we tried to establish a relationship between a white parish in Johannesburg and a Dominican black parish in Soweto. When the parishioners from Soweto were invited to come and share the 10 am Mass in Johannesburg, they accepted with delight, but they were scandalised to find that when they arrived at 2pm, all the white people had given up and gone home!

The final thing that I will mention is the insecurity of the poor. In this liquid fluid world, human ties are temporary. This is true at work and in the home. The average American male has eleven jobs in his working life. For everyone this implies unpredictability. For the rich nomads it can imply unexpected openings, opportunities to be grabbed rapidly, to exploited before one moves on. For the immobile, then it can imply weakness. The insecurity dissolves the old solidarities of the working class. Trade unions lose their power to resist. Labour solidarity evaporates. I quote Bauman again, 'Once the employment of labour has become short-term and precarious, having been stripped of firm (let alone guaranteed) prospects and therefore made episodic, when virtually all rules concerning the game of promotions and dismissals have been scrapped or tend to be altered well before the game is over, there is little chance for mutual loyalty and commitment to sprout and take root.'[15]

The Last Supper presents us with a moment of supreme insecurity and liquidity. The bonds of the community are dissolving. In this situation Jesus gives the disciples his body once and for all, without reserve. The Risen Lord will tell them

15. Op. cit., p. 148

'Behold I am with you until the end of time' (Mt 28:20). In a fluid world, Christianity should embody a fidelity, of once and for all commitment. Thomas Aquinas reminds us that religion comes from a word, *religio*, which means a bond. We are bound to God and to each other. Making vows, remaining faithful, expresses something essential about our relationship with God, in marriage or religious life.

Surely this is a fidelity to each other that we must embody within the Church. Chrys McVey was for many years a missionary in Pakistan. He wrote that the missionary does not just unpack his suitcases, he throws them away. He comes for good. It is true that Chrys did have to find and re-pack his suitcases and that was because he was summoned to Rome by the Master of the Order, which is a pretty good excuse. In fact he has just been in Ireland with him! I was often deeply impressed by brethren and sisters who left home and gone abroad to just be with another people for the rest of their lives. For St Thomas Aquinas, courage is above all endurance. It is hanging in there, when it may seem pointless. It is the courage of staying put, as a sign of God's fidelity.

Surely we may hope to live something of that in our relationships with people who are marginalized. In the world of development and in religious life, there are fads and fashions. I overheard one general superior in Rome saying that 'Latin America is out and Asia is in. Liberation theology is a bit old hat now; inculturation is the new thing.' Aid agencies are looking elsewhere. When Eastern Europe was opened up, then Africa dropped further down the priorities. When major institutional donors make grants these days, they usually wish to know what are our exit strategies. One must not hang along. Of course priorities change, crises arise and sometimes pass, but surely we must be in for the long haul.

I must stop. I have not, I must admit, been able to offer you a 'spirituality from the margins.' Only someone who has lived on the edges could do so. Instead I have glanced at a few forms of marginalization, in terms of information, power, identity and spatial exclusion. There are others, such as that of women which I have not mentioned, especially inside the Church. I want to suggest that faced with these the Eucharist offers a wisdom, that of God, in whom the centre is everywhere and the periphery is nowhere. This is our home. We can be at home nowhere else.

Participants' Responses

CAROL DORGAN LSA [Ed.]

KEY INSIGHTS CALLING FOR A RESPONSE

This talk found a deep resonance within many, which was clear from the Flip Chart "shorthand". A number of quotations, or at least, phrases used by the speaker were recognizable as groups got down to their work and grappled with the task of responding to the given questions. A variety of ideas was expressed. The circumstances of poor people, and newer – perhaps less obvious - forms of their marginalization in today's world were highlighted. An example mentioned by several groups was the lack of access that poor people worldwide have to the World Wide Web, through lack of technology and lack of computer literacy. They are disconnected from networks of communication and information, and we know today, that access to information means access to power. In fact it has been argued that today, social structures have been partially replaced by information structures, and so the ownership of information is becoming more important than the ownership of things such as machinery, land, real estate. On the other hand, the wealthy suffer the impoverishment of superficial, brief encounters in place of more lasting relationships as a consequence of having such a high degree of mobility. They could, in fact, be called the new nomads. Power means mobility, and poor people cannot move around at will. But if, in an Irish town or city, costs become too high or environmental requirements too strict, the enterprise can easily move to China or Mexico.

With regard to ourselves, being truthful demands that we

need those on the margins to tell us who we are. They do not hide who they are, and, unlike the rest of us, have little to lose. The first Eucharist, the Last Supper, saw Jesus sharing a meal with his disciples in an 'upper room' while outside on the streets the religious authorities, in collusion the military power of the state, were about to capture him. In this safe place he reveals his deep love, and finds a way to continue nourishing his followers through what will be an ever- living memorial by means of the ordinariness of bread and wine. Bread making involves gathering in the ingredients and kneading the dough by the rhythm of a two-fold movement: bringing the dough into the centre and then spreading it out. This process can signify inclusiveness, and certainly not marginalization. Unlike the military might of the state, the power that Jesus represents is found in the sign that he himself was, the signs that he performed, and the sign that he became in the broken and shared bread. Jesus, speaking words of truth before Pilate, refusing to resist with violence, accepting his death sentence with supreme dignity after a life spent healing and speaking of his Father, submits to the powerlessness of crucifixion as a criminal. Yet we know that this apparent defeat was followed by Resurrection. Since we are often faced with the enormity of finding effective responses to many social problems it was encouraging to be reminded that 'small is beautiful', and that simple gestures and actions which seem insignificant can have a powerful effect as signs, speaking of a deeper reality. They are God's currency, as attested to by numerous examples in the Bible. This provoked some of the religious present to ask themselves: what kind of sign do we present today? What reality do our lives signify? We live in an information age, but the wisdom necessary to deal with all this is seriously lacking. The Last Supper reveals a wisdom that is a counter-force to today's increasingly divided world and questions the prevailing exercise of power looked upon as might and control. It's inclusiveness symbolism is a symbol of the unity of all humanity. Jesus gives himself for everyone without exception, yet according to one group, our experience of Eucharistic celebrations rarely matches these deep realities.

WHAT ACTIONS WOULD PROMOTE THESE INSIGHTS?

To come up with specific actions seemed more of a challenge this time after such a rich and wide-ranging talk, and some suggestions tended to be more general, and aspirational rather than concrete. Several groups highlighted the significance of the Eucharist and its prophetic possibilities for inclusion of the marginalized. But how to make it more meaningful for those who are so distant from Church activities and have little sense of belonging? Indeed, how make it a more meaningful celebration for ourselves? Several people acknowledged their own need for a deeper grasp of the meaning of Eucharist so that its celebration can then be richer and more inclusive. Enabling marginalized people to have access to computers was also taken up. Then there was a feeling among a number of participants that they themselves needed to draw closer to the experience of poor people, face up to our own poverty of resources as well as our wealth, reach out and listen more to those on the bottom rung of the ladder, and be more attentive to how we actually *live* the Gospel. The silent witness of life can often speak more powerfully than words.

Some *small signs* were suggested, ways of living that could be a relevant message today: exercising leadership as a form of service rather than as an exercise of superiority; forming groups for reading and praying the Scriptures following the *lectio divina* model;[3] preparing inclusive liturgies that use inclusive language; setting times aside in own busy work schedules for analyzing with others what we are doing, reflecting on it in the light of the gospel, and then allowing the fruits of that collective effort to inform our work. This would help us to critically evaluate what we are already doing, and the resources we are already using. It would also check the chronic activism that characterizes almost all our effort, and can hinder the lasting effectiveness of what we are aiming to do.

---

3 *Lectio divina* is an ancient, monastic way of reading the Bible text which has been revived today. It involves reading a short passage of the Bible, and finding a word or phrase that speaks to our lives. The idea is to allow that word or phrase to become our food for the day, nourishing thoughts, words, actions.

Study Questions

Spirituality from the Margins

*"The poor today are not so much the disposed as the discon-
nected...... (F) aced with these multiple marginalisations, the
Church offers a Eucharistic wisdom".*

1. These two key points lie at the heart of this paper.
    What are the 2 or 3 main points in the paper which
    resonated within you?

2. Take each one; try to explain it to another person.

3. Looking again at each of these points focus on one,
    and ask yourself, 'What are the implications of this
    wisdom for my life?'

4. Having looked at the implications, consider what are
    the one or two practical steps you need to take to
    begin to integrate this wisdom into your life?

5. Imagine you have consistently sought to integrate
    this wisdom into your life by fidelity to these practical
    steps. Ask yourself, 'What new developments do I
    see in my relationship with God and with people who
    are marginalised?'

If you wish to give more time to reflect on the issues raised in this
paper the questions above may help you. They are also intended
to help group discussion on this topic. As a preparation for
group discussion participants are encouraged to reflect on the
questions privately.

Feedback and comments are welcome by the CORI Justice
Commission, Bloomfield Avenue, Donnybrook, Dublin 4.

3

Spirituality for Social Engagement

ENDA DINEEN AND DONAL LINEHAN

WHAT IS IT?

We asked two professional people working in two of the most disadvantaged areas of Cork City recently why do you do this kind of work? (They are both Christian but not Church going) One answered spontaneously but jokingly 'my mortgage.' However she is a person who has previously worked in the Third World. Her spirituality is of human development. The second person said, 'I grew up in a poor family and something in me wants others to make it just as I have done.' She is currently putting the finishing touches to a PhD.

We believe there is a spirituality for social engagement whatever our belief. Different circumstances call for different responses. The particular circumstances of our time cannot be separated from our spirituality.

There is always someone or something to make us stop and reflect on what we claim to believe, what goes on deep inside us, for example:

- People sleeping in doorways
- People who have to wait longest for hospital treatment
- Young people who have dropped out of school and who end up on drugs or alcohol and ultimately in jail
- Travellers hidden behind big boulders
- Run down flat complexes where if you dare to go you see young and old living in appalling conditions. The flat complex in the glen is one such place where people only go to live as a last resort.

A Force From Within

People respond in different ways to these types of situations. One such response is a denial that this poverty exists. 'There is no poverty; there is plenty of cash around. These people are lazy. They are parasites, letting the rest of us work so they can get social welfare. Why can't they get up and work?'

The other response comes from deep inside one, like 'this need not be so. Why do I have and they don't? Why do others have more than enough and these people struggle to exist? Why is there a persistence of poverty in a culture of plenty?'

Spirituality of justice is a *driving force from within* towards social engagement. It's a way of seeing. It incorporates acting justly, analysis of present reality, collaboration with others and right relationships. Only CORI could put it so concisely! It's a caring presence, being with people and working with people. It's a commitment to analysis, sharing and empowerment.

For Social Engagement

Ronald Rolheiser in his book *The Holy Longing: The search for a Christian Spirituality* tells the story, now well known and perhaps also known to you:

> 'Once upon a time there was a town built beyond the bend of a river. One day children from the town playing by the river noticed three bodies floating in the water. They ran for help and people from the town quickly pulled the bodies from the river.
>
> One body was dead so they buried it. One alive, but very ill, so they put that person in hospital. The third was a healthy child so they placed it with a family who cared for it and took it to school.
>
> From then on a number of bodies came floating down the river and every day the good people of the town would pull them out and care for them, taking the sick to hospital, placing children with families and burying the dead. This went on for years, each day each day brought it's quota of bodies, and the people of the town not only came to expect a number of bodies each day but worked at developing

elaborate systems for picking them out of the river and tending to them. Some of the people became quite generous in tending these bodies and a few extraordinary ones even gave up their jobs so that they could tend to this concern full-time. The town itself felt a certain pride in its generosity.

However during all this time and despite all the generosity and effort did anyone think of going up the river, beyond the bend that hid from their sight what was above them, and find out why every day, these bodies came floating down the river?'

Work downstream means taking time to be close to the person/ family in their woundedness, desperation, fear and confusion. It means being a friend rather than a patronising person. It also means taking time to work out solutions together, to cry and laugh together. It involves providing services as we see in the story. We are very familiar with the great services that have been provided and still are being provided by voluntary groups. However at times because of pressure in providing the service there is neither time nor energy to look up stream to analyse. However this must be done. In providing any service it takes a long time to convince any relevant government department of the tremendous need out there.

Look for example at the situation of ex-offenders. Where do these people come from? How is it that more than 90% come from poor families in poor areas? Why have they dropped out of school? Why do they do drugs? Why are they violent? As we look up stream we see social partnerships and social inclusion units. However, the media headline says €100m and 100 acres for a jail to hold 1,000 offender. Is this the only solution?

Back again to the story, as well as providing the service what else do we need to do? Resources have to be put into empowering people, working with people, making them part of the solution. Advocacy is essential. As far back as the 70s and 80s when a more socially minded theology was being developed the Church was urged to move beyond the caring services into a commitment to a just society. "Justice does not happen- it has to be worked for" (*The Work of Justice,* 1977).

WHERE GOD IS EXPERIENCED

God is revealed in the two great commandments of loving God and loving other people – as we love and cherish ourselves. (Lev 19:18, Mt 22:35-40) Jesus set forth this mutual concern as the witness to being his disciples. 'By this love you have for one another everyone will recognise that you are my disciples" (Jn 13:34-35) Moreover he launched his ministry by proclaiming the good news to the poor and broken-hearted (Lk 4:18). His explicit concern for the marginalised conveyed how God sees a dignity within each person that is not expressed in terms of social status. Jesus identified with the marginalised: '…as long as you did good to the least of my brothers and sisters, you did it to me' (Mt 25:40).

The letters of John emphasise that this love has to be 'real and active' as distinct from words and talk (I Jn 3:17-18). James applies this concern to people's need for clothes, food, payment for work and to preferential treatment for people who are well dressed (Jas 2). Wealth has responsibilities beyond providing comfort and luxury. Indeed Jesus has warned against becoming addicted to riches and against a self-serving and domineering exercise of authority. His model of leadership and authority is to serve rather than to be served (Mt 20:28).

The genuine worship of God was understood to require social justice in the Old Testament and the abuse of riches and power made the sacrifices unacceptable before God (Amos 5:8). 'My servant is endowed with my spirit to bring true justice to the Nations' (Is 42:1-4) Moreover, the people of God were frequently reminded of God's special care for the widow, the orphan and the stranger and this was enshrined in the welfare customs in those times (Deut 24:17-21). The core of what God wants is that his people 'act justly, love tenderly and walk humbly with God' (Micah 6:8). This is 'a faith that works through love' (*The Work of Justice*,1977).

The call to human fulfilment and to the transformation of the world is the new commandment of love. Human progress can contribute to true happiness even though it is often frustrated by self-aggrandisement, malice and a distortion of values.

The spirit of God works for liberation from corruption so that all the earth's resources can serve the development of people and become an offering acceptable to God. 'The gifts of the spirit are diverse. He calls some to bear witness clearly to the desire for heaven and to keep that desire alive among people. Others he calls to devote themselves to serving humanity here – a ministry which provides material for the kingdom of heaven' (*Gaudium et Spes*, the Church in the World, pars. 38, 36-39).

Thus far, spirituality is presented as a driving force of vision and values on how we respond to need. At a human level, it calls for a caring presence in working with people, vulnerable people (downstream) and leads on to a courageous commitment to analysis and advocacy for just structures (upstream). Moreover, God is revealed and experienced in these caring relationships and in the work of justice. Social engagement is a human dynamic which can be enriched powerfully by the Christian spirit: "that you may have life and have it to the full' (Jn 10:10).

AT THE CUTTING EDGE

The Church has a remarkable record in education and care services and in outreach to the poor. Personnel and funding were invested with generosity and the forward planning was very impressive. There is so much evidence in services, buildings, developments, training. It is important to note, however, that these services were undertaken in the context of evangelisation. The primary purpose was to safeguard, spread and foster the faith rather than to combat social inequality or to reform society. All Church activities and services – schools, hospitals, care services, scouting – were instruments of socialisation into religious belief and practice. The Church was central in the control and resourcing of these care services – inevitably carrying human failings in the exercise of power and responsibility.

What Tony Fahey says in the book *Social Policy in Ireland* (1998), is interesting and challenging especially to those of us who belong to religious congregations. He talks at length of the Catholic Church's major contribution to providing social services in Ireland in the nineteenth or twentieth centuries. However he also says 'the Church's larger impact in the development of social policy and social administration was limited.'

Today, as we all know, the situation is very different. Falling numbers in religious congregations no longer make it possible to continue its provision of social services (even though still a lot is being done). However, Fahey goes on to say that even though numbers have fallen and hence providing services is limited religious can still be at the 'cutting edge of social policy.'

Back to our story then: the work of looking up river and doing serious analysis in order to be able to influence public policy has a huge impact on the shape of future development and cannot be left undone.

The Church and its agencies are only one player among many in today's rapidly changing society. Moreover, the Church's influence and resources have declined in face of humanistic and materialistic values, declining members, scandals involving Church personnel and institutions. Power is more widely distributed in society and the expectation of civic entitlement tends to replace christian charity.

In this scenario, there is a strong temptation for the Church (dioceses and religious institutions) to withdraw from social care in this new secular and humanistic context. This would be to concentrate its limited resources in promoting 'communities of faith' where traditional values and practices can be preserved. It would seek to preserve religion from the corruption of humanistic and secular values (Murray 1990).

A SOCIAL CHARTER

Today social care and education are seen as a human and civic entitlement and as making a claim on the State and on the goodwill of voluntary organisations, without the strings of religious control or civic control. This is a noble aspiration since the poor tend to be marginalized and controlled by the structure of society (e.g. in education). There is a deeper respect for the freedom of the person as an expression of worth and potential. Moreover, when we engage with and enable another person to grow from within, we promote that deeper connectedness and bonding that is social inclusion.

These noble expectations are countered, however, by the materialistic culture in which success is measured in terms of wealth, status, mobility, consumer choice. An unbalanced focus on economic development is likely to give generous rewards and incentives for the 'work and enterprise ethic', leading to a widening gap between the powerful and the poor. The lack of attention to the poor in the media and their low visibility in society are features of an affluence that lacks a social charter. People are valued more for what they have than for inherent dignity and belonging in society.

Thus the challenge for genuine human values and for social engagement is real and urgent and the call to transform society is the 'new commandment of love' (*Gaudium et Spes*, The Church in the Modern World, 1965, par 38).

The Church is clear that human progress can contribute to true human happiness but is also well aware how vanity and malice can destroy solidarity. Human progress has the potential for good but can also be confounded into destructiveness. In so far as it can contribute to a better ordering of society, it contributes to the building up of God's kingdom of justice and peace.

The Church offers the human race a sincere cooperation in establishing a universal solidarity in keeping with the dignity of each person. She is moved by no earthly ambition and wants only to be led by the Holy Spirit to carry on the mission of Christ who came to save and not to judge, to serve and not to be served. (*Gaudium et Spes*, Church in the Modern World, 1965, par. 3, 39). Thus Christian agencies are called to engage in the world as it is with an overlap of human values and christian vision.

SPIRITUALITY WITHIN THE HUMAN

Spirituality has been associated traditionally with the interior life and the practices of prayer, penance and obedience. Much energy is invested in the promotion of devotional practices as experiences of belonging in the Church, and of closeness to God. The hymn *Soul of my Saviour* expresses the feeling of gaining inner strength for living in a hostile world. The focus is on being citizens of heaven and on remaining somewhat unattached to the human. What is human and secular is also addictive and corrupting, calling us away from God by offering its own inherent satisfaction.

Christian spirituality today is centred within the human journey and in an integration of body, mind, heart and spirit in each person. It focuses on the network of human relationships - with ourselves, with other people with the environment — in the circumstances of our time. It relates to experience and engages the whole person in the various stage of development so as to empower and transform one's life. It is a way of living the Gospel with due attention to the requirements of justice and solidarity. The Spirit of Christ sends us to being the good news to the poor (Luke 4:18). Thus it is securely based on the Scriptures and, especially, on the pattern of Christ's ministry (Downey, 1997, ch. 5 and 7).

Christ took to himself our human journey, thus creating a bond with every person. The Word of God was made flesh and came to live among us; working with human hands, thinking with a human mind, acting with a human will and loving with a human heart. This bond is deepened in the sharing of his Spirit with us. Hence he could say: 'I was hungry and you gave me to eat' (Mt 25). He sets the pattern of our journey to God through and beyond the human.

Such a pattern of spirituality requires a continuing interaction between engagement and contemplation, work and prayer. This is essential if we are not to miss the meaning and depth that are available in human interactions. Social care points to the prayers of discernment, desperation and celebration at the unfolding of God's kingdom with its inner power to grow and as the treasure hidden by consumer rubbish (Mt. 13:31, 44; McVerry, 2003).

We can experience and know God within our relationship with other people and the world around us. God's voice and presence can be felt in the search for truth, in the need for goodness, the hunger for freedom, wonder at the beautiful and the voice of integrity. (*Redemptor Hominis,* John Paul II, par 18) *Ubi caritas, ibi Deus est.* Loving and caring attention to one another can prepare the way for an intimate relationship with God:

I sought my God but could not find him
I sought my soul but it evaded me
I sought my neighbour and found all three.

Social engagement is a valuable form of pre-evangelisation for our time. Many expressions of religious faith lack roots and credibility for younger people. Attention is required to the search for relationships and for life's meaning through human experience, if religious belief and belonging are to have fresh vitality. (Gallagher, 2001, p. 120-121). The following are some of the signs of the times:

• Wonder and respect before another person,
• Hearing the cry of the poor,
• Recognising Christ in the poor and marginalized;
• Realising that the kingdom of God is happening here and now while it reaches its fulfilment in heaven.

The Eucharist is the summit of all the activity of the Church and the fountain from which its energy flows. It does not exhaust the entire activity of the Church, which is called to work and to pray that the whole of society became the Kingdom of God. Perhaps, this integration of prayer and care might be better expressed in devotional practices – a challenge to creativity! (*Sacrosanctum concilium*, Constitution on the Sacred Liturgy, 1965, par. 9- 10).

RECENT MODELS

Love moves us to a concern for the wounded and marginalized. Edmund Rice, Catherine McAuley and Nano Nagle, were strongly motivated by an urgent call to social care and social justice. The lack of education and life skills for the marginalized was of urgent concern. So also was the importance of helping poor families to benefit from education. They turned to the Bible for inspiration in regard to social justice and then made their commitment. The spiritual ethos of Catherine McAuley's new institute gave to care for the poor and the orphaned through shelter, education, employment. She also took account of the whole person, including fun and dancing. Catherine counselled her sisters to see their concern for and service to the poor as the basic source of self sacrifice and penance.

The following are some of the implications of a human engagement with a Christian vision:

- the commitment to a caring presence among the marginalized and a practical involvement with them;
- recognition of the inherent demands and frustrations of working with wounded and hard-pressed people as thespiritual cost of loving care (I Cor 13:4-7);
- personal integrity of the carer to be maintained through self-care, appropriate training and creativity, ethical values, a generous heart and deep prayer;
- accountability for resources, service delivery and outcomes;
- enrichment of local communities in the bonds of belonging and linking with them;
- working for the kingdom of justice and peace is seen as a truly spiritual enterprise.

Social engagement offers opportunities for heroism and creativity. The names of Bob Geldof (World Aid), Adi Roche (Chernobl children) , Fr. Niall O' Brien (Child Enslavement), Victor Bewley (Traveller Community), Mother Teresa (Homeless people), Sheila Holland (Psychiatric care) come to mind.

As a nurse therapist, Sheila Holland saw each and every long-stay psychiatric patient as a unique person with potential and with his/her own story to tell. 'She created a therapy unit in the hospital where people could squiggle their toes in real sand, sit by a pond with real fish, sing a song, paint a picture, and, above all else, feel part of a real and loving community' (*The Irish Examiner*, County news Supplement, 27 April, 2004).

Today, projects sponsored by dioceses and religious orders include a majority of lay workers in positions of responsibility. There include professional workers and volunteers. Moreover, these agencies tend to engage more in social analysis and advocacy and in influencing public opinion, e.g. CORI, SVP and Trócaire. This is the new culture of service and influence but without the power to control.

Religious are making a further contribution by setting up Care Trusts to continue the ministries of service and advocacy through genuinely human values as a Christian witness to the God within and beyond the human.

STANCE WITH THE POOR

A spirituality of social engagement envisages a genuine presence with the wounded and the marginalized as the basis for advocacy on their behalf. Agencies are needed to provide independent analysis and a supportive voice in the assessment of need and of resource allocation. A sharper focus is desirable on care programmes as counter to the forces of neglect and of social control today. Of course, this role caries the risk of hostility and rejection by the establishment. Finally, it is essential to work in alliances with other people and agencies with a shared commitment. (*Gaudium et Spes*, the Church in the Modern World, 1965; The Work of Justice, 1977; Prosperity with a Purpose, 1999).

Effective advocacy today would seem to require that several links be joined in a chain of credibility:

- Real stories and working with people
- Competent analysis
- Focus on shared values
- Making alliances and proposing ways forward
- Mobilising public opinion and political support
- Negotiating with competence and courage.

WHY STAY WITH SOCIAL ENGAGEMENT?

Social engagement is fulfilling and challenging at the human level. It brings a good buzz, a sense of adventure, good friendships and a strong sense of purpose in working for and with people. There is a feeling of having some power to do good. It can offer a self-transcending experience – to grow in nobility and to face the corrupting forces in ourselves and in human institutions.

It is a spiritual calling for volunteer and professional workers alike, for policy makers and agency personnel, for people of goodwill whether they want to enrich human citizenship or christian fellowship or both.

Care and concern are ways of participating in the mission of Christ and the Church. The kingdom of God is essentially about the quality of our relationships. Today we need a greater clarity that the Church's mission of evangelisation includes the development of people through the values of practical care, social planning and the work of justice. These are authentic human values and are also a form of pre-evangelisation to a fuller experience of God. In this work, the Church's influence goes beyond its members when they engage in shared action with other religions and people of goodwill.

God revealed Jesus and his mission on Mount Tabor in a powerful and splendid vision and the disciples found it 'good to be there'. Then they had to come down from the high experience and face back into the messy world of social engagement.

BEATTITUDES FOR SOCIAL ENGAGEMENT

Blessed are you,
    when you remain available, sharing in simplicity what you possess.
Blessed are you,
    when you weep over the absence of happiness around you, and throughout the World.Blessed are you,when you opt for gentleness and dialogue even when this seems long and difficult.
Blessed are you,
    when your creativity devise new ways of donating your time, your tenderness and gems of hope.
Blessed are you,
    when you listen with your heart to detect what is gift in others.
Blessed are you,
    when you strive to take the first step,   thenecessaryone to attain peace with brothers and sisters throughout the world.
Blessed are you,

when you keep in your heart wonderment,
openness and free questioning of life.
Blessed are you,
when you take seriously your faith in the Risen Christ.
– Louise Helene Renou

REFERENCES

Gaudium et Spes, The Church in the World of Today (1966): II
Vatican Council document 'Gaudium et Spes'

Sacrosanctum concilium, Constitution on the Sacred Liturgy (1966):
II Vatican Council, Chapman, London.

Downey, Michael (1997): Understanding Christian Spirituality,
Paulist Press, New York.

Dorr, Donal (1984):The Spirituality and Justice, Gill &
Macmillan, Dublin.

Fahey, Toney (1998): The Catholic Church and Social Policy, in
Sean Healy and Brigid Reynolds (eds): Social Policy in Ireland, Oak
Tree Press, Dublin

Fuller, Louise (2002): Irish Catholicism Since 1950 – The undoing
of a Culture, Gill and Macmillan, Dublin.

Gallagher, M.P. (2001): Dive Deeper, Barton Longman & Todd,
London.

Jerusalem Bible, Dorton, Longman and Todd, London

Jesuit Centre for Faith and Justice (2003): Windows on Spirituality, Columba Press, Dublin

John Paul II (1979): *Redemptor Hominis,* Redeemer of Man.

McVerry, Peter (2003): The Meaning is in the Shadows,Veritas, Dublin

Murray, Donal (1990): Secularism and the New Europe, Veritas,
Dublin

Prosperity with a Purpose (1999): Irish Bishops Conference,
Veritas, Dublin

Renou, Helene, 'The Beatitudes' in the African Missionary
Magazine (No.3 Easter 2004) The Society of African Missions, Cork.

Rolheiser, Ronald (1999):The Holy Longing: The Search for a
Christian Spirituality, Doubleday, London.

Whelan, C.T. (Ed) (1994): Values and Social Change in Ireland,
Gill and Macmillan, Dublin

Work of Justice (1977): Irish Bishops Pastoral, Veritas, Dublin

Participants' Responses

CAROL DORGAN, L.S.A. [Ed.]

After the third presentation the group process was slightly amended to include a final question that would enable participants to say what they would take away from the day.

KEY INSIGHTS CALLING FOR A RESPONSE

Perhaps the most common insight arising from what the speakers said was that our spirituality is distorted. 'The reason there is so much injustice is because our spirituality is wrong,' declared one group. We need a 'new spirituality' that is much more closely integrated with human, everyday experience, with literally 'finding God in all things' – in all of creation. Spirituality is about right relationships at every level of our existence. An integrated spirituality also means that we engage and grapple with the problems of social injustice, not only with the consequences, but also with the causes. There is a circular movement here: an authentic, integrated spirituality nourishes social engagement and helps to avoid burn-out, while social engagement enriches and colours our spirituality.   Several groups seized upon the phrase 'a chain of credibility': all authentic critique of society will be based on clear, factual, analyses, which presuppose a a certain kind of formation and preparation, as well as a genuine presence among the marginalized, and all is to be seen as part of spirituality.   In speaking of analysis and preparation, many highlighted the indispensable place that the CORI Justice Commission held, especially through all the educative and tireless advocacy work of the Justice Office, which provides much needed support to so many communities and groups throughout the country.

WHAT ACTIONS WOULD PROMOTE THESE INSIGHTS:

Education and formation to read and critically comprehend our social situation is one clear form of action needed. Not many of us are prepared or sufficiently informed to grapple with the complexities of causes, despite the ongoing work of informing and forming carried out by the CORI Justice Office. When we do manage to work on causes it is difficult to stay the course without a supportive group environment and an adequate spirituality. We need to continue to support CORI and continue to gather together others who would be our allies in this work, raising awareness of issues and sharing and disseminating CORI material. With such groups we might be able to begin articulating a new spirituality, which finds God in nature, in other people and in the ordinary and extraordinary events that make up daily life. As a visible part of Church, we need let go of the almost ingrained need to be in control, and become more ready to listen, learn, support and empower others. And then came the final question:

WHAT WILL I TAKE AWAY FROM TODAY?

There was a very enthusiastic response to the Conference, both to its content and process. That economics can be a part of spirituality, and have a basis in values was an exciting new realization for some. The speakers jolted people's awareness both of present-day challenges of living justly, and of the need to find an adequate spirituality for 'the long haul.' This last will find its basis in the Gospel, nourished by more meaningful Eucharistic celebrations, and it will be the fruit of community analysis and reflection on the life experience of the marginalized. Even if we feel very small and powerless in face of the needs, small actions and gestures can have a powerful impact. God works through what is small and seemingly insignificant.

Religious found themselves questioning what kind of witness they were giving today: too comfortable? Too distant from the experience of poor people? Many of those present expressed new energy and enthusiasm to respond to this challenge and find new ways to narrow the gap.

For all, the questions around *values*, both those which are espoused, and those which are actually expressed in contemporary Irish society, were central. In this respect many took up the ideas proposed earlier in the day by Dr Eamon O'Shea, about a National Fairness Strategy and a national debate on values.

Finally, the large attendance revealed the great level of interest among many people and groups around the country in the quest to bring social action and spirituality together for a more enriching spirituality and a more reflective and effective social action.

Study Questions
Spirituality for Social Engagement

A spirituality is described in this chapter as 'a driving force from within towards social engagement.'

1. What are some of the elements of this spirituality?

2. Share your understanding of a spirituality of justice with one or two others.

   Note how sharing expanded your own understanding.

3. What are one or two practical implications of trying to live such a spirituality?

4. Describe the vision, values and practices which nurture a spirituality of justice.

5. How does a growing spirituality of justice change your life?

If you wish to give more time to reflect on the issues raised in this paper the questions above may help you. They are also intended to help group discussion on this topic. As a preparation for group discussion participants are encouraged to reflect on the questions privately. Feedback and comments are welcome by the CORI Justice Commission, Bloomfield Avenue, Donnybrook, Dublin 4.

Afterword

Spirituality might be defined as a faith vision of life, but it is a vision incarnated in life. It is a lived reality, embodying a set of values. For us who follow Jesus, it means being guided by his values and example. Life and spirituality are not separate entities, as spirituality incorporates all of life. It is not a case of praying on Sunday and preying on others for the rest of the time.

Our creative God shares creativity with us and calls for a response. The chosen people were reminded that the promised land was God's gift – they did not own it! St Paul reminds us that all is gift (I Cor 4:7). If that is our starting point, it will give us a radical base for justice and fairness, as it will root them in love and gratitude. Ultimately, love is the basis of life and relationship; justice in the true sense is love and seeks to express that. Grateful people do not have difficulty sharing.

I want to thank our speakers for the rich contributions to today: It was encouraging to hear Eamon O'Shea and Brendan Kennelly, as economists, indicating the need for some spiritual base for economics. There is need for more than a market approach.

Timothy Radcliffe was rich as usual, broadening our horizons of poverty and offering new perspectives to further our ongoing reflection.

Enda Dineen and Donal Linehan gave us the fruits of many years at the 'coal face.' It is a service that could not have continued without a strong spiritual base. They have been able to find life in the unlikely places, knowing God is in the midst of all.

A word of thanks is due to all who made today possible. To the facilitators, to Seán, Brigid, Theresa, Bernadette, Phyllis and the many who worked behind the scenes, sincere thanks. This is a dialogue that is to continue to bring the Gospel and the world more together in love, justice and truth.

MICHAEL DRENNAN S.J.
CORI Secretary General

Contributors

Eamon O'Shea and Brendan Kennelly

Dr Eamon O'Shea is a senior lecturer in the Department of Economics at NUI, Galway . Dr O'Shea has made a significant contribution to health and social care research in Ireland in the past decade. His latest book, *Policy and Practice for Dementia Care* in Ireland has recently been published by Ed Mellen Press.

Brendan Kennelly is a lecturer in the Department of Economics at NUI, Galway. His research interests are health economics, welfare economics and social policy.

Timothy Radcliffe O.P.

Timothy Radcliffe studied theology at Blackfriars, Oxford. In 1992, he was elected Master of the Dominican Order. Now based once more in Blackfriars, Oxford he is much in demand as a lecturer and preacher all over the world. He is author of *Sing a New Song* (Dominican Publications, Dublin), *I Call You Friends* (Continuum, London).

Enda Dineen and Donal Linehan

Sr Enda is a Mercy Sister living and working in Cork City. A Primary School Teacher in an inner city school in Cork for a number of years, she went to Peru and worked in poverty stricken areas for ten years.

Fr Donal Linehan is Parish Priest in Ballinora near Cork. Donal was co-founder of a number of organisations, including *Ogra Chorcai* (Cork Youth Association). Donal is also author of *Community Involvement Mayfield,* a 1985 publication.

Both Enda and Donal began work in Mayfield in the early 80s, where very few structures were in place to cope with young families growing up in large housing estates and very rundown flat complexes.